THE
HEALING
JOURNEY

THROUGH ADDICTION

THE
HEALING
JOURNEY

THROUGH ADDICTION

Your Journal for
Recovery and Self-Renewal

Phil Rich, EdD, MSW
Stuart Copans, MD

John Wiley & Sons, Inc.

NEW YORK ✦ CHICHESTER ✦ WEINHEIM ✦ BRISBANE ✦ SINGAPORE ✦ TORONTO

This publication is designed to provide accurate and authoritative information in
regard to the subject matter covered. It is sold with the understanding that the
publisher is not engaged in rendering professional services. If legal, accounting,
medical, psychological or any other expert assistance is required, the services of
a competent professional person should be sought.

Library of Congress Cataloging-in-Publication Data:

Rich, Phil.
     The healing journey through addiction : your journal for recovery and
self-renewal / Phil Rich, Stuart Copans.
          p. cm.
     ISBN 0-471-38209-4 (paper : alk. paper)
     1. Compulsive behavior — Patients — Rehabilitation.   2. Substance abuse —
Patients — Rehabilitations.   3. Diaries — Therapeutic use.   4. Self-care, Health.
I. Copans, Stuart.   II. Title.
RC533 .R53 2000
616.86'03 — dc21   99-088272
Printed in the United States of America.
10 9 8 7 6 5 4 3 2 1

To Mary, Laurie, Roy, Jon, and Ben, who help me remember what life is about.

    —STU

To Bev and Kaye, who allow me to be totally myself.

    —PHIL

Contents

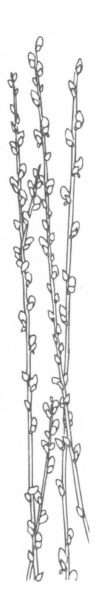

Preface: About *The Healing Journey Through Addiction*   ix

1. Embarking on Your Journey   1

2. A Road Map Through Addiction   13

3. Destination: BEYOND DENIAL—AWAKENING AND ACKNOWLEDGMENT   43

4. Destination: UNDERSTANDING YOUR ADDICTION   63

5. Destination: THE PRESENT—THE PRICE YOU PAY   77

6. Destination: GETTING SUPPORT   93

7. Destination: ADDICTION-FREE—THE DAY YOU STOP   117

8. Destination: RELAPSE AND SLIPS   125

9. Destination: UNDERSTANDING EMOTIONS   147

10. Destination: THE PAST—UNDERSTANDING PERSONAL HISTORY   163

11. Destination: SELF-INVENTORY   187

12. Destination: SELF-ESTEEM AND PERSONAL IDENTITY   205

13. Destination: UNDERSTANDING RELATIONSHIPS   221

14. Destination: GOOD HEALTH—REBUILDING BODY,   239
    MIND, AND SPIRIT

15. Destination: UNFINISHED BUSINESS   261

16. Destination: THE FUTURE—MAINTAINING RECOVERY   277

17. As One Journey Ends, Another Begins   291

Acknowledgments   295

PREFACE

About *The Healing Journey Through Addiction*

ADDICTIONS COME IN all shapes and forms. Although it's become popular to think of almost *any* behavior that has a compulsive quality as an addiction, for our purposes an addiction is a dependency on a substance, activity, or relationship that pulls an individual away from everything else in the world. It is characterized by desires that consume people's thoughts and behaviors and is acted out in habitual activities designed to get the desired thing or engage in the desired activity (addictive behaviors). Unlike simple habits or consuming interests, addictions are dependencies whose consequences can seriously impair, negatively affect, or destroy relationships, health (physical and mental), and the capacity to function effectively. Most of all, an addiction is debilitating.

In the end, addicts are dependent on that thing that dominates their thoughts and desires and directs their behaviors; pursuit of that thing becomes the most important activity in their lives. In the advanced stages of addiction, nothing is as important as the addiction itself. For this reason, no matter what the addiction, the object of desire may rightly be called a narcotic: a substance, activity, or relationship that soothes and numbs.

The Healing Journey Through Addiction is written for those who have an addiction or display clearly addictive behaviors. The addiction can be a dependence on alcohol, drugs, prescription medications, gambling, food, sex, tobacco, or any number of other things or activities that serve to absorb the attention, deplete the energy, damage the health, and often exhaust the relationships of the addict. Sometimes popularly described as a disease, addiction is an illness that affects not just the addict but those closest to the addict and society as a whole as well. Addiction is truly a community illness.

"Obstacles cannot crush me / Every obstacle yields to stern resolve / He who is fixed to a star does not change his mind."
—LEONARDO DA VINCI

You've picked up this book or someone has given it to you for a reason. Possibly you have an interest in addictive behaviors and dependence, or you're concerned about someone else. More likely, someone believes or suspects that *you* have an addiction. However you came by this book, *The Healing Journey Through Addiction* is intended for those people who suspect, believe, or know they have an addiction and who want to take steps to regain control over their lives and relationships.

The Healing Journey Through Addiction isn't a guide to the treatment of addiction, and it doesn't prescribe a particular method or approach for overcoming or treating addiction. There are many excellent resources for both self-help and professional help in dealing with addiction and dependent behaviors, and there are several models that define addiction and its treatment. *The Healing Journey Through Addiction* isn't intended as an alternative or replacement for getting help or treatment. Instead, it is a guided personal journal and workbook that will help you understand your addiction, your life, and your choices; it is a resource that will help you figure out for *yourself* how best to deal with your dependence.

This book will guide you along your journey as you deal with your addiction and help you recognize the pitfalls, side roads, and dead ends along the way *before* you take them. This is a journal to help you avoid the living death that addiction can bring and return you to living life.

THE
HEALING JOURNEY

THROUGH ADDICTION

I

Embarking on Your Journey

> *"It is not heroin or cocaine that makes one an addict, it is the need to escape from a harsh reality. There are more television addicts, more baseball and football addicts, more movie addicts, and certainly more alcohol addicts in this country than there are narcotics addicts."*
> —**SHIRLEY CHISHOLM**

The Healing Journey Through Addiction is really not about addiction; it's about recovery. Although you'll find information about addiction and addictive behaviors in these pages, your journey is one of recovery and restoring your life. All journeys have a starting point, destination, and map. Your journey starts with understanding and identifying your addiction, and each destination point along the way represents an increasing understanding and a step toward the deep recovery that marks the end of the journey.

Addictions have been studied and written about by many people, and there are many different ways to understand and make sense of addictive behaviors. Some people see addiction as a disease in which addicts have little power over the cause or onset of addiction. Others see addictive behaviors as a choice and addiction as the outcome of this choice. In this vein, the writer Philip K. Dick commented, "It is a decision, like the decision to step out in front of a moving car. You would call that not a disease but

an error of judgment." But in either case—disease or decision—recovery is possible.

Some see addiction as a character trait or predisposition (the so-called addictive personality), whereas others see addiction being acquired through exposure to the addictive behaviors of others (such as family members). In the case of physical addictions, such as alcoholism or drug dependence, many believe the susceptibility to be dependent is passed on genetically. Others believe that addiction is simply the result of repetitive behavior that in some people leads to a *physical* dependence and reliance (such as alcohol, caffeine, or nicotine dependence) and in others to a *psychological* dependence. Although not all addictions are physical (gambling, for instance), they are truly just as addictive and destructive as their physical counterparts.

However acquired and whether physical or psychological, we know that addiction can be overcome and the addict "cured." *The Healing Journey Through Addiction* will help you to understand your own addiction, make sense of its causes and history, and figure out how best to overcome the power of your addiction and enter your own version of recovery.

Your journey is one of recovery and restoring your life.

Recovery Work

The freedom from addiction is typically referred to as recovery. Some people believe that full and complete recovery is possible, whereas others believe that the addict is never fully recovered but always in recovery, guarding against relapse and the possibility of slipping back into addictive behaviors.

Your Recovery Journal

The Healing Journey Through Addiction is a guided journal and a workbook that will help you learn about, deal with, and work through addiction and the tasks of recovery. In addition to providing important information and direction that will help you move from addiction to recovery, your recovery journal will provide a place for you to think about your life, explore and express your thoughts and feelings, and record your experiences along the way.

In its most basic form, a journal is a way to record the details of your life and develop a memoir of your experiences and thoughts. A journal can also be a special companion—a part of yourself that exists outside of you in which you share your feelings, your ideas, your worries, and your successes. Beyond this, a journal can be a place to explore and express your thoughts and feelings, reflect on the way you interact with the people and things that surround you, and experiment with new ideas. Journal writing is a means to record and better understand how you approach life and how you *want* to approach life.

A guided journal, such as this one, goes one step further: it introduces you to journaling and provides structured journal entries that will help you to discover and express your feelings, frame your thoughts, and experiment with different journaling styles and techniques. Ultimately, a journal can be a valuable companion along a deeply personal road.

Journal writing is a means to record and better understand how you approach life and how you want *to approach life.*

Using *The Healing Journey Through Addiction*

If you're working with a counselor or other health care professional, she or he may assign a specific chapter or journal entry for you. If you're working on your own, where should you begin?

The Healing Journey Through Addiction is designed to be used in the sequence presented; the progression of chapters and journal entries coincides with the stages most typically associated with recovery, starting with actively addictive behaviors and moving toward full recovery. But not everyone picking up this book will be at the same stage in their addiction or their recovery. For this reason, each chapter can stand on its own and be used independently of all other chapters. You can choose the order best suited to your needs. The next chapter, "A Road Map Through Addiction," will help you assess where you are in your recovery work and help you pick the best place to start your healing journey.

Moving at the Right Pace

Abstinence (not engaging in addictive behaviors) and recovery (overcoming the addiction) are not the same thing, although they are certainly related. . . . True, sustainable recovery is the result of really learning and living out the tasks and life changes required to overcome addiction.

Although you may want to glance ahead, don't try to rush through this book. Just as you can't fully recover from addiction overnight, you shouldn't try and complete your journal in a day or two. *No matter how quickly you work through each chapter, or the book as a whole, you cannot be assured of recovery unless you have really taken in, integrated, and applied the work required on this journey of recovery.* For some, the journey to recovery is a short trip; for others, it is a journey that takes place one step at a time over many months and even years. Many believe that recovery is a journey that never fully ends. Some people who appear to recover discover that it is only too easy to slip back into addictive behaviors at a later time. Be cautioned then, that simply *completing* the work in this book doesn't necessarily result in recovery—recovery comes from *living* the work and the lessons learned.

Abstinence (not engaging in addictive behaviors) and recovery (overcoming the addiction) are *not* the same thing, although they are certainly related. Although abstinence is a step in the right direction, it alone does not equal recovery. There is no "right" pace for full recovery. True, sustainable recovery is the result of really learning and living out the tasks and life changes required to overcome addiction. The *right* pace is the pace at which you're able to make and integrate the necessary changes.

As you complete each chapter, ask yourself if you've *really* completed the work in that chapter. If you can honestly answer that you have, then you're ready to move on. If not, then you should return to the work of that chapter, or earlier chapters, and do the work again. As you complete each chapter, reread and think about what you've written before moving on to the next phase of your recovery work.

It may not be possible or desirable to work through *The Healing Journey Through Addiction* in the sequence presented. You may come to a chapter or an entry that you aren't ready for. If so, skip it and come back to that chapter or entry at a later point in your recovery work. You may also want to move in a different sequence because of an immediate need to deal with pressing emotional or life issues. However you choose to use this book, read Chapter 2 before continuing on to other chapters.

Making Yourself Comfortable

You may not be used to keeping a diary or journal and perhaps feel unsure of how to best start. First, regardless of the chapter or entry you start with, decide which conditions and environment will best support your journal writing. Here are a few suggestions that may help make the process more comfortable and productive for you:

- Set aside a regular schedule for working through your journal, preferably at a time of day when you're fresh and have the most energy.

- Take breaks during your writing if you need to. Stretching your legs can also give your mind a break.

- Think about the kind of environment that will best suit and support your writing. Consider playing some quiet music or other relaxing background sounds, for instance. Would you prefer a brightly lit room filled with sunlight or a room subtly lit by candles?

- Make yourself physically comfortable. For many, writing is enhanced by the comfort of a favorite chair or the feel of a comfortable piece of clothing.

- Pick a place to read and write that will be emotionally comfortable for you as well. Do you prefer a quiet private location or a public community area?

- If writing is emotionally difficult for you, or you find your feelings or thoughts overwhelming at times, consider having a comforting picture or object nearby or something else that might be emotionally comfortable.

- Make sure there's someone available for you to talk to after you write, if you think you may need some personal contact or support.

- Once you've completed an entry, reread it. Reflecting on what you've written can help you gain new insights.

Make sure there's someone available for you to talk to after you write, if you think you may need some personal contact or support.

Using the Entries

The styles for different journal entries in *The Healing Journey Through Addiction* vary, and each entry is provided only once. There are some entry formats that you may especially like using, and you'll find some entries you'll want to repeat. Feel free to keep a supplemental journal in addition to this book where you can add your "spillover" thoughts or write additional entries. You may also want to photocopy certain blank entries in order to return to that entry again.

Each journal entry ends with a Things to Think About section, a series of questions for you to consider after you've completed your entry. These aren't a formal part of the entry but are reflective points that may spark a further journal entry, serve as discussion points if you're sharing your experience with a counselor or a friend, or simply act as a focal point for your thoughts.

Sharing Your Experiences and Getting Help

For most people, recovery work and all that it entails is inherently difficult, and the act of exploring and writing about painful thoughts, feelings, behaviors, and relationships—past and present—may be uncomfortable. Some entries in *The Healing Journey Through Addiction* may evoke difficult and painful feelings, which may make you feel vulnerable. Seek help whenever you find yourself feeling especially pained, fragile, or lost. A support network —a counselor, self-help group, family, friends, neighbors, members of your church or temple, or others in your community—is essential during your recovery work.

The Value of Your Recovery Journal

Much of the benefit of any journal comes as you gain skills in reflection and self-expression. As you answer questions or write your thoughts in a journal entry, you're having a "conversation" with yourself. Even if you have a problem expressing your thoughts and feelings to others, writing can be cathartic, allowing you to unburden yourself in private. The main thing is that you *are* expressing what you think and feel. It can help you understand what you need at whatever stage in the process you find yourself.

Your recovery journal can be of great value as you work through your addiction and approach recovery. Your journal can help you understand the issues that led you to addiction and build order out of the emotional turmoil that has resulted from it. But its usefulness depends directly on you: it can only be an important tool in your recovery work if you use your journal on a regular basis.

Your Experience with Addiction

In many ways your experience with addiction is similar to that of millions of others who have experienced addiction before you. But despite the similarities, your experience remains unique, and there are no pat and simple answers or methods for getting clean and staying addiction-free. This is *your* addiction, and so you must learn for yourself where it comes from, what keeps it alive, and how best to overcome it and restore your life to normalcy. In fact, one of the reasons for keeping a personal journal is because addiction—no matter how common—is a very personal affair.

Your addiction is not only destroying your life, but it is also damaging your family, your friends, and your community as well.

Although your addiction is unique and personal, it is not only destroying *your* life, but it is also damaging your family, your friends, and your community as well. Your recovery and renewal is theirs also.

Starting at the Beginning

Although *The Healing Journey Through Addiction* is a good resource for people interested in learning about addiction, it is written for people with addictions. It can be read by anyone but completed only by someone who has an addiction or engages in addictive behaviors.

Not everyone picking up this book is ready to face their addiction. In fact, a common feature of addiction is denial, or the dismissal or rejection of the idea of a personal addiction. The first step essential for recovery is the *acceptance* of a problem. The first journal entry in this book will allow you to think about why you're reading this book and help you decide what you're going to do with it.

All journal entries require a level of personal honesty that may sometimes be difficult to give. The first entry is no exception. Remember that these entries are for you and you alone unless you choose to share them with someone else. Every journey has its first step. This is yours.

HOW DID YOU GET THIS BOOK?

1. How did you get this book? Check off the answer that is *most* accurate.

___a. *I got this book for myself.*

___I *know* I have an addiction.　　___I *think* I may have an addiction.

___I'm concerned about myself.　　___I want to learn more about addiction.

___I'm worried about someone else.　　___I want to try to appease people who

___I stumbled across it.　　　　　　keep bothering me about addiction.

___other: _____

___b. *Someone else gave me this book.*

___I'm not sure why.　　　　　　___They're trying to upset me.

___They *believe* I have an addiction.　　___They *suspect* I have an addiction.

___They're concerned about me.　　___They want me to change my behaviors.

___They're nosy.　　　　　　　　___They want to control my life.

___They think I should learn about　　___They thought I might be interested
　addiction.　　　　　　　　　　in it.

___other: _____

2. Think about how and why you got this book.

a. If you got the book for yourself, how honest are you being with yourself about why you got it? _____

_____

_____

_____

_____

_____

b. If someone gave this book to you, take the time to ask this person why.
What was his or her answer?

_____

_____

Was he or she being honest with you?

_____

_____

How do you feel now that you know (or can guess) why it was given to you?

_____

_____

_____

3. What are your goals for this book? Check off all statements that apply, and add any additional goals you may have.

___I don't have any goals.

___I want to decide whether I have a
    problem.

___I want to function more effectively.

___I want to get my addiction under control.

___I want to get people off my back.

___I want to prove to others I don't have an addiction.

___I want to prove to myself I don't have an addiction.

___I want to learn more about addiction.

___I want to quit my addiction com-
    pletely.

___I want to make other people happy.

___I want to read the book.

___I want to save my relationships.

other: _____   _____

_____   _____

4. In what way is your possession of this book meaningful to you?

_____

_____

_____

5. This book was written for people with addictions. How does it apply to you?

_____

_____

_____

_____

_____

THINGS TO THINK ABOUT

- Were you being honest with yourself? If so, was it difficult to be honest?
- Are you in denial of a problem, or are you ready to begin your journey?
- Can you do this on your own?

2
A Road Map
Through Addiction

PAUL

I thought my life got off track after some pretty big problems at home and a divorce. I was drinking and smoking heavily, significantly depressed, and really unable to be productive at work. In fact, things got steadily worse.

I'm lucky because people at work stuck by me, and a world of support opened up. I didn't accept it easily, but once I did and got help things started to improve bit by bit and day by day. Later I realized my life had gotten off track before my divorce and that my addiction went back years. I thought that the loss of my wife, my kids, and my house drove me to drink, but it was really the other way round. My addiction led to the loss of my life.

That was years ago. I needed some direction to get things back on track and somebody to point the way, and luckily I got it. I'm still recovering from all those years of abuse, and so is my family, but I'm doing so much better now. And I decided to really make addiction my life—I'm an addiction counselor myself now.

An addiction is truly a biopsychosocial phenomenon, affecting physical, mental and emotional, vocational, and interpersonal functioning.

AN ADDICTION IS truly a biopsychosocial phenomenon, affecting physical, mental and emotional, vocational, and interpersonal functioning; that is, it affects people's lives at every level. Addiction, then, is no "damn *private* hell." It reaches out to consume those around the addict: the victim of the drunk driver or that victim's family, the addict's own family, and society at large through the financial costs accrued from physical illness and lost health, crime, lost work hours and underproduction, lost income and bankruptcy, accidents, suicides, violence, and mental illness, to name a few.

Addiction knows no boundaries. You're kidding yourself if you think that addictions develop only in people who are poor, undereducated, of low morals, antisocial, or somehow on the fringes of society. People of wealth and renown have long been the victims of drug and alcohol addiction, and benzodiazepines (such as Valium and Librium) were once commonly popularized as the suburban middle-class addiction of the 1960s. Among the professions at the highest risk for substance abuse and addiction are physicians and nurses. Similarly, among those with credit cards and other forms of fiscal credit available to them, behaviors that resemble addiction involve overspending and the accumulation of huge debt and result in social relationships and lives in near ruins. Few people today doubt that the use of tobacco and caffeine are addictions that run across all strata of society. Alcoholism, drug abuse, sexual addictions, overeating and undereating, medication abuse and dependence, and gambling are addictive behaviors that are found at all levels of social class, wealth, education, culture, and morality.

Understanding Addiction and Dependency

Defining addiction is not simple. People often associate addiction only with substance abuse, but addictive behaviors can go far beyond that. The key to addiction is an obsessive and compulsive need or dependence on a substance, object, relationship, activity, or some other thing. Note that the emphasis is on the person's response, desire, and need for a thing, *not the thing itself*. Thus it's possible to say that a person can have an addiction to virtually anything.

Given this, it's important to understand the behaviors that can be considered addictive. These are the things that addicts do in order to fulfill cravings and satisfy the emotional or physical needs of the addiction. Essentially, there are six clear indicators of an addiction:

1. *Object of desire.* In an addiction, there always exists an object of desire. This is the substance, thing, activity, or relationship that drives the addiction, whether it be alcohol, food, sex, gambling, pornography, drugs, or anything else that can spark obsessive ideas and drive compulsive interest or use into addiction.

2. *Preoccupation.* There is an obsession with the object of desire, a need for the thing that drives the addiction. Obsessions are thoughts, ideas, and impulses that pop up and occupy a great deal of emotional and mental energy.

3. *Driven behaviors.* A compulsion to reduce the cravings and satisfy the obsession with the object of desire drives the behavior of the addict into planning for, seeking out, and using the substance or engaging in the activity.

4. *Loss of control.* Between obsessive thoughts and compulsive behaviors, the addict loses personal control over thoughts, feelings, ideas, or behaviors when it comes to the desired thing. Even when addicts try to stop or cut back on addictive behaviors, they fail. This is the hallmark and a central defining feature of addiction and dependence.

5. *Dependence.* There is a dependence, physical or psychological, on the object of desire; only the object can satisfy the

In an addiction, there always exists an object of desire.

Physical *dependence results from daily, repeated use of alcohol, certain drugs and medications (heroin and benzodiazepines), and other substances such as nicotine and caffeine. . . .* Psychological *dependence always accompanies addiction, and even where there is no physical addiction there is a very real emotional dependence on the drug or activity.*

desire and fulfill (at least temporarily) the addict. *Physical* dependence results from the daily, repeated use of alcohol, certain drugs and medications (heroin and benzodiazepines), and other substances such as nicotine and caffeine. In absence of these substances, the addict not only feels emotional distress and discomfort but also physical symptoms of withdrawal as the body has come to need the substance for its daily functioning. These physical symptoms of withdrawal range from mild effects such as discomfort to serious and life-threatening symptoms such as seizures, which can only be prevented through continued use of the substance or a substitute. *Psychological* dependence always accompanies addiction, and even where there is no physical addiction there is a very real emotional dependence on the drug or activity (It is believed that there is no *physical* dependence on cocaine, for instance, but the psychological dependence is quite real, as are the effects of psychological withdrawal. Similarly, there is no physical dependence on gambling, but psychological dependence is completely evident and has ruined many lives). On the psychological level, without the "fix" provided by the object of desire, the addict experiences mild to severe emotional mood swings and other emotional impairment or distress.

6. *Negative consequences.* An important final characteristic of addiction is the harmful consequences of the addiction. Typically this is the biopsychosocial effect in which addictive behavior results in harm or negative effects on physical or mental health, interpersonal relationships, or social or economic functioning. Although a person might seem "addicted" to reading, television, or food, or even another person, the behavior is only rightly considered addictive when there is a harmful consequence. Without causing such harm, the behav-

ior may well be antisocial, self-defeating, or self-destructive, but it may not rightly be considered an addiction in the true sense.

The American Psychiatric Association generally defines conditions such as substance dependence (and substance abuse, which the association considers one step below dependence) and gambling as persistent and maladaptive patterns of behavior that lead to significant impairment or distress. These diagnoses are usually indicated by, among other things, an inability to stop the activity despite knowing there are harmful consequences; damage to important social, occupational, or recreational activities; and the frequent inability to feel satisfaction without engaging in the activity.

Functional Impairment

One important measure of addiction lies in the level of current functioning or risk to effective function in one or more of the major life domains: physical health, mental health, social relationships and interactions, occupational functioning (work or school), and economic well-being.

The risk of damage in any one of these areas is one of the effects of addiction that is both a defining feature of the addiction and a consequence. Even in the case of tobacco use, which has little immediate impact on function, the smoker faces the long-term possibility of health loss and life-threatening illness and therefore physical and probably financial dysfunction in the event of a serious illness. In other words, addicts always either lose their ability to function effectively in an important life domain or willingly risk the possibility.

Addicts always either lose their ability to function effectively in an important life domain or willingly risk the possibility.

The Continuum of Addiction

Addicts don't become addicted overnight. There is a progression as people first engage in the behaviors and experiences that may later become addictions. If the substance or activity is capable of creating a dependency, then there is a risk of addiction with repeated use over time.

For most addictions a form of tolerance is created through use, in which more and more of the substance or activity is required to feel the "high" or emotional satisfaction that the addiction brings. In the full-fledged addict, the addiction may simply bring a sense of *normalcy,* offsetting physical or emotional distress more than providing a high. In other words, the addict has to use (or engage in the activity) just to feel normal. This is what dependence truly means.

Accordingly, there is a continuum of addiction, ranging from preaddiction to the advanced stages of addiction and dependence. The progression from use into addiction can be measured in two ways.

1. The effect that addictive behaviors have had on effective and healthy personal functioning, ranging from mild impact to severe

Minor
Impact

Major
Impact

●——————————————————————————————●

IMPACT ON FUNCTIONING

2. The intensity of cravings for the substance, activity, relationship, or thing, ranging from mild and infrequent cravings frequent and intense cravings

Few and/or
Mild Cravings

Frequent and/or
Intense Cravings

●——————————————————————————————●

CRAVINGS/NEED FOR OBJECT

When taken together, these two measurements can help people who engage in addictive behaviors gauge their progression into addiction.

Use the next journal entry to explore and measure your own journey into addiction.

ADDICTION THERMOMETER

Impact on Functioning

1. On this 1 to 5 scale, circle the number that most approximates the effect and impact that your addictive behaviors are having on any major area of your life, including physical or mental health, relationships, work or school, financial, legal, or any other area of expected and usual functioning.

Minor Impact				Major Impact
1	2	3	4	5

2. Using the scale in Question 1, rate the impact of your use/addictive behaviors in each of these individual areas. Leave blank if not applicable.

__emotional stability	__legal	__romantic relationships
__family relationships	__mental health	__social interactions
__financial	__overall functioning	__work or school
__friendships	__physical health	__work relationships

other: _____   _____

_____   _____

3. In which three areas are your addictive behaviors leading to the greatest problems?

a. _____

b. _____

c. _____

4. What do the ratings that you gave tell you about the effects of your addictive behaviors on your ability to function effectively?

_____

_____

_____

_____

5. What do the ratings that you gave tell you about the effects of your addictive behaviors on your life?

_____

_____

_____

_____

Cravings and Needs

6. On this 1 to 5 scale, circle the number that most approximates the intensity of your cravings or needs to use or engage in addictive behaviors.

Few and/or Mild Cravings				Frequent and/or Intense Cravings
1	2	3	4	5

7. Are your cravings more physical or psychological?

_____

_____

8. Do you ever refuse to give in to your cravings? If so, what happens when you go without satisfying the craving?

_____

_____

_____

_____

9. What does your Addiction Thermometer tell you about your level of addiction?

_____

_____

_____

_____

THINGS TO THINK ABOUT

- Are your addictive behaviors affecting your life more than you previously imagined or were willing to consider?
- What have you learned about yourself, your behaviors, and your habits through using the Addiction Thermometer?
- What is it like to have to examine your behaviors and habits in this way?

Abstinence, Moderation, and Recovery

Although there are many prescriptions for recovery and the treatment of addiction, there are nevertheless essentially just two ways to stop addiction. The most common and widely accepted idea is lifetime abstinence, or the complete cessation of the addictive behavior. In this model, the addict never again uses the substance or engages in the addictive activity. Of course, abstinence is a viable option only with certain addictions. It would be impossible, for example, for a food addict never again to engage in eating, and it would probably be unhealthy for a sex addict never again to have a sexual relationship. This leads to the second model for overcoming addiction.

Often, the addiction *will determine the appropriate recovery model. The food addict must eat; hence moderation, not abstinence, is called for. But in many cases, the decision must be made by the* addict.

Many alcoholics and drug abusers, gamblers, and other addicts are unwilling to give up their addiction. For them, the goal is to continue using the substance or engaging in the behavior without letting the substance or behavior control their lives. For other addicts, though, this is an unachievable goal. For them, recovery requires complete and lifetime abstinence.

Often, the *addiction* will determine the appropriate recovery model. The food addict must eat; hence moderation, not abstinence, is called for. But in many cases, the decision must be made by the *addict*. You will have the opportunity to do just this as you work through this book. However you choose, remember that neither abstinence nor moderation equal recovery; they are merely the first steps. Recovery is not the simple cessation of addictive behaviors. It is the process that addicts pass through as they learn to deal with their addiction and the state they reach as they eventually overcome the addiction and build a new life—and a new *framework* for life. In recovery, people are rebuilt and renewed, as are their self-image, behaviors, relationships, and skills.

Before you move further into your recovery work, use the next entry to think about exactly what it is you're addicted to.

NAME YOUR POISON

1. Choose a word or a short phrase that describes what you think you may be addicted to. It can be a substance, an activity, a relationship, a behavior, or anything else that is prompting you to read this book.

_____

_____

2. Now write a sentence including that word or phrase. The sentence can be about anything as long as it contains the brief description you supplied in Question 1.

_____

_____

_____

3. *My addiction . . .* _____

_____

_____

The Continuum of Recovery

Just as addiction doesn't develop overnight, neither will you enter into and remain in recovery in a single step. People enter their recovery at one point, and by the time they are considered fully recovered they have undergone a major transformation. Although many believe that recovery is a never-ending process (that is, there is no such thing as "complete" recovery for an addicted person because there's always the risk of relapse), it is nevertheless true that the person deep into recovery has made significant personal, emotional, and behavioral changes and is living a different life than when addicted.

Although your experience with recovery will be intensely personal, there are five fairly typical stages through which addicts pass on their journey to and through recovery. These range from early awareness of addiction (a prerecovery stage) to acceptance of the problem and the resolution to do something about it to the development of new ideas, behaviors, and lifestyle that supports and maintains addiction-free behaviors and relationships. Within each stage are specific emotional and psychological tasks that must be worked through completely before you can move on to successfully complete the tasks of the next stage.

Although these stages are a predictable part of the recovery process, recovery doesn't always move in a straight line and not everyone successfully negotiates and accomplishes the tasks and challenges of each stage. For some people, recovery is straight-

There are five fairly typical stages through which addicts pass on their journey to and through recovery. These range from early awareness of addiction (a prerecovery stage) to acceptance of the problem and the resolution to do something about it to the development of new ideas, behaviors, and lifestyle that supports and maintains addiction-free behaviors and relationships.

forward, a continuous move from addiction to nonaddiction. For others, it is a journey filled with side roads and dead ends that can easily lead back into addictive behaviors and active addiction. It is a difficult road to take and usually requires a great deal of determination and a significant support system to provide the guidance, help, and encouragement you'll need. Take heart, though: it is a journey that many have completed successfully and a journey at whose end you'll be stronger, wiser, and more confident in your skills and abilities.

It's also not always clear exactly what stage a recovering addict is in. The stages tend to flow together and fluctuate, and people sometimes take those side roads that can cause a setback on their journey. During this journey, emotions seesaw and behaviors change. With recovery, there's always the chance that just when you think you've mastered your addiction, a thought, an interaction with someone, a memory, a bad day or a good day, or any number of other "triggers" can send you back into emotional turmoil and down one of those side roads or dead ends.

Unlike other life journeys through transition (such as the passing from adolescence to adulthood, parenthood, menopause, retirement, and bereavement), the journey away from addiction and to recovery has no defined end. For some, it's a journey that takes weeks. Others will need to guard against relapse for the rest of their lives. Recovery is a different kind of journey from the natural and expected life passages; it is a journey of self-determination and self-change.

While you work on accomplishing the goals of each stage, you must also take care to avoid the side roads and dead ends that lead you back to addiction.

The Five Stages of Recovery

The stages of recovery will help you understand what lies ahead in your healing journey. Each stage has defined tasks and goals. To successfully tackle and accomplish the tasks and goals of later stages, it is important to first master the tasks and goals of the early stages. They provide the foundation and the cornerstone for your journey. While you work on accomplishing the goals of each stage, you must also take care to avoid the side roads and dead ends that lead you back to addiction.

STAGE 1: AWARENESS AND EARLY ACKNOWLEDGMENT

Stage 1 is really the prerecovery stage that paves the way for the beginnings of serious recovery work. The stage begins with a dim, but growing awareness that you may indeed have a problem with addiction.

At this point, you are actively using or engaging in addictive behaviors and are preoccupied with getting, using, or engaging in those behaviors. Because of social pressures (or illegality), these behaviors are illicit and hidden. Quite likely family members and friends are complaining, unhappy, or nagging you about your behaviors. You may be frequently annoyed at them for bothering you and dismiss or deny their concerns. Prior to and during this stage, there are often significant functional problems, and in fact people are often pushed into this early stage of awareness by the concerns of family or friends, a health issue, financial issues, a work problem, or a legal matter.

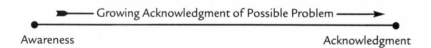

Awareness   — Growing Acknowledgment of Possible Problem →   Acknowledgment

The end of this stage is marked by a growing acceptance of a problem with addiction, and an acknowledgment that some action is needed to further address issues.

Tasks of the Stage

The tasks during this prerecovery stage involve a general shifting of perspective from outright denial and dismissal to a willingness to do the following.

- Accept the *possibility* that you are addicted.

- Consider the point of view of other people about your behaviors.

- Look at your functioning in life areas such as physical and mental health, work or school, relationships and social interactions, finances, and other important areas (including legal issues).

- Stop dismissing the concerns of others, denying all problems related to addictive behaviors, and insisting everyone else is wrong.

Side Roads and Dead Ends

It is all too easy for those dependent on an addiction or a particular way of doing things to slip back toward old behaviors. It is very difficult to change. The recovery road is full of temptations and every conceivable reason to return to the old ways. These are either dead ends that lead nowhere or side roads that lead back to addiction. In this early and fragile stage, these include:

- *Denial.* The unwillingness to see or consider that there may be a problem and the inability to acknowledge the truth

- *Dismissal.* The personal decision to reject and simply dismiss the views of others, and even concrete evidence of an addiction

- *Disbelief.* The unwillingness or inability to believe that personal behaviors or problems could be symptoms of an addiction

Denial, dismissal, and disbelief amount to covering your eyes and ears—the refusal to believe there may be a problem and the pretense that there isn't one.

Alone or taken together, denial, dismissal, and disbelief amount to covering your eyes and ears—the refusal to believe there may be a problem and the pretense that there isn't one. These side roads allow addiction to continue.

STAGE 2: CONSIDERATION AND INCUBATION

Although Stage 2 also is a precursor to actual recovery, in many ways it's the first concrete step toward that process. Flowing from the acknowledgment that marks the completion of the tasks of Stage 1, this stage opens with a willingness to further explore and consider ideas about addiction and recovery. The primary movement during this stage involves increasing knowledge about the realities of addiction and the impact it's having on your own life and on the lives of others.

Consideration   Decision to Stop

If the work of this stage is characterized by incubation (or the development of new ideas), then its end is defined by the *hatching* of the idea: an acceptance of the problem and the decision to stop or moderate addictive behaviors.

Tasks of the Stage

The tasks of this stage center around broadening your perspectives and your ability to uncover your eyes and unplug your ears.

- Listen to others around you and take their concerns seriously.

- Look hard at the consequences of your behaviors, both to yourself and to other people.

- Think about what might happen if you modified or stopped the behaviors that concern people around you or have caused you problems.

- Recognize that your addictive behaviors are not moving your life in a positive direction and are more likely counterproductive, dysfunctional, and actively interfering with your life.

Side Roads and Dead Ends

It is easy to get derailed on this journey, especially in these early stages of recovery. Now that you've begun to move away from blind denial toward considering how your addiction affects you and how to stop or moderate your addictive behaviors, it's all too easy to slip backward because of:

It's far easier to stay addicted than to get into and stay in recovery.

- ✦ *Failed abstinence/moderation.* During this stage it's not unusual for people to experiment with abstinence or, reluctant to give up their addiction completely, to try to moderate it. But without new behaviors and relationships that can substitute for the addiction or a plan to prevent relapse, it's very easy for newly recovering people to give up on their efforts and simply slide back to their usual addictive behaviors.

- ✦ *Renewed denial.* Addicts often have low tolerance for frustration and are accustomed to quick fixes for feeling good—that's the nature of the addiction. It's still very easy, and quite common, for people barely in recovery to slip right back into denial.

- ✦ *Loss of interest.* It's always hard to change behaviors. This side road is related to the New Year's resolution that's quickly forgotten after a few days. It's far easier to stay addicted than to get into and stay in recovery.

STAGE 3: EXPLORING RECOVERY AND EARLY ACTIVITY

By now, you're more committed and entering the first clear stage of recovery. Beyond denial, Stage 3 unfolds with a clear resolution to quit the addiction and the recovery work during this stage of development involves exploring the ideas and activities of abstinence, moderation, treatment, and recovery. During this stage, people actively move toward stopping the addiction and move out of experimenting with the idea of recovery. Treatment of one kind or another begins, and by the completion of the stage, people have truly entered recovery and are committed to overcoming the addiction. A concrete foundation for a successful and lifetime recovery is laid.

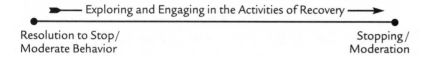

Resolution to Stop/
Moderate Behavior

Stopping/
Moderation

Tasks of the Stage

The tasks to be accomplished during this stage set the pace for later and deeper recovery and assure that recovery becomes lifelong. Lifetime recovery means never returning to addiction.

- Learn about and engage in some form of active treatment.

- Learn to cope with the emotional, social, and other realities, demands, and difficulties of daily life.

- Learn about and develop a plan to prevent relapse.

- Participate in activities and relationships that substitute for the addiction.

Side Roads and Dead Ends

- *Relapse.* One reality is that of slipping back to addictive behaviors. Even though it's always possible to regain recovery after a slip, an early relapse can lead to a lack of motivation and a sense that it's not possible or not worth staying clean.

- *Giving up.* It's difficult to change old behaviors and very difficult to live without an addiction, especially when many addicts have not fully developed alternatives to their addiction. People in early recovery are experiencing many feelings that may have formerly been masked by their addiction and are almost certainly going to experience physical or emotional withdrawal and the sense of discomfort that comes with withdrawal. It's very easy for people in early recovery to give up and return to their addiction.

- *Disillusion.* It's difficult to change. After a slip back into addiction, a particularly difficult day, an emotional storm, or an exposure to the reality of life without addiction, it can be very easy for emotionally raw newly recovering people to feel helpless and disillusioned with their own skills, motivations, and willpower. It's normal to feel this way, but if not attended to these feelings can be a direct path back to old behaviors.

STAGE 4: EARLY RECOVERY AND REHABITUATION

It may seem like slow going, but recovery means more than simple abstinence or moderation. It is a change in perspective, attitude, values, and lifestyle. It is a process that remakes the addict, renewing and restoring life. Stage 4 marks the entry into full, but *early,* recovery. Recovery is still fragile, but this is the stage that most solidifies recovery, during which a new life is built.

Early Recovery — Development of New Behaviors — Commitment to Recovery

Stage 4 opens with recovery in its early stages, and its end is marked by a commitment to *lifetime* recovery, having learned the skills, developed the behaviors, adopted the habits, and built the relationships needed to maintain a lifetime of freedom from the addiction.

Tasks of the Stage

- Avoid the people, situations, and activities that may serve as triggers to relapse and addictive behaviors.

- Develop behaviors that support mental and physical health, enhance social functioning, and produce positive results.

- Restore and build new relationships that support recovery.

- Engage in satisfying activities that positively substitute for addiction and support recovery.

Side Roads and Dead Ends

- *Overconfidence.* The trap during this stage may come in the form of overconfidence and the mistaken belief that the addiction is a thing of the past. This can lead to slips back into old behaviors, in the mistaken belief that addiction is conquered.

- *Relapse.* Relapse will continue to threaten an addiction-free life for many years ahead (forever, for some). Slips do happen, though. Accordingly, it's important for people at this and later stages in their recovery to understand that relapses do not negate change and good work, and they are not a reason to fully relapse and give up those gains.

- *Despair.* Following a relapse, it is easy for people in early recovery to feel worthless and/or unable to maintain a life free of addiction. Relapse can lead to despair, and this can lead to further relapse. Giving in to despair is a shortcut to readdiction.

Overconfidence can lead to slips back into old behaviors, in the mistaken belief that addiction is conquered.

STAGE 5: ACTIVE RECOVERY AND MAINTENANCE

Stage 5 is recovery proper. For many, Stage 5 has no ending because recovery is a lifetime process. Others believe that it is possible to be fully recovered from an addiction. Either way, it is certainly difficult to mark an end to the stage, as actively maintaining your recovery really "unfolds" into the life you will live for many years to come, with renewed relationships and a restored spirit, addiction free and able to make your own choices.

By the time you enter Stage 5, you are actively monitoring

yourself, your feelings, your thoughts, your behaviors, your activities, and your relationships. As you work through the tasks, you are living out all that you have learned as you ensure that each day is an addiction-free day.

Self-Monitoring → Maintaining Safe Behaviors → Self-Regulation

Stay tuned to your thoughts and feelings, and maintain a healthy self-awareness.

As you near the end of this stage, having largely accomplished its tasks and overcome its challenges, you will be *constantly* regulating your life.

Tasks of the Stage

- Recall daily the lessons learned from your addiction and through your process of recovery.

- Ensure that you're engaging in safe behaviors, activities, and relationships.

- Stay tuned to your thoughts and feelings, and maintain a healthy self-awareness.

- Take charge of and be responsible for your decisions at every level.

Side Roads and Dead Ends

- *Disregarding.* Even in this late stage of recovery, relapse is a possibility. Forgetting the lessons learned, believing addiction is forever a thing of the past, or simply letting go can be a side road away from recovery.

- *Relapse.* At any stage, a slip is possible and at any stage a relapse can send even the most recovered individuals back into addictive behaviors. Even if a relapse occurs, don't let it lead you away from a return to recovery.

- *Low self-esteem.* Many addicted people suffer from poor self-image and low self-esteem, and a slip or relapse after months or years of addiction-free living can reduce self-esteem even more. It's always important to recognize these events and feelings as commonplace and thus not allow them to pull down all the great work accomplished. Responding to poor self-esteem by returning to old behaviors is one of the side roads back to addiction.

Your Journey

Restoring and rebuilding your life after addiction is a painful and arduous process that takes place only over time. How much time will depend on your commitment to recovery, your personality, your approach, and your resilience, to name but a few of the factors that influence recovery and support personal renewal. Few people can go this route alone; the support of family, friends, and the community is critical.

There are no shortcuts on this journey. Some people will enter recovery with ease and negotiate the stages smoothly, quickly moving from one to the next. Others will struggle each day with the major issues raised by recovery, and some will never enter recovery at all. However, recovery is possible for everyone.

The work you do in this journal will help you understand recovery, the journey you're taking, and most importantly, yourself. You may already have begun your journey, or you may be right at the beginning wondering how best to begin it. The journal entries in this chapter will help you pinpoint where to begin and what tasks are most pertinent at this point. The next entry will help you gauge where you are in your journey, and the entries later in this chapter can help you decide where best to start your journaling work.

Some people will enter recovery with ease and negotiate the stages smoothly, quickly moving from one to the next. Others will struggle each day with the major issues raised by recovery, and some will never enter recovery at all.

CHECKPOINT: STAGES

Based on the descriptions in the preceding pages, circle the letter that most closely describes your personal experience with recovery.

	I'm not yet ready to deal with this.	I'm now ready to deal with this.	I'm past this point.
Stage 1 Experiences: Awareness and Early Acknowledgment			
Accepting the possibility of addiction	A	B	C
Considering the point of view of other people	A	B	C
Willing to look at personal health and social functioning	A	B	C
Stop dismissing the concerns of others	A	B	C
Stage 2 Experiences: Consideration and Incubation			
Taking the concerns of others seriously	A	B	C
Looking hard at the consequences of your behaviors	A	B	C
Considering impact of stopping behaviors that concern others	A	B	C
Recognizing that addictive behaviors are counterproductive	A	B	C
Stage 3 Experiences: Exploring Recovery and Early Activity			
Learning about and engaging in some form of active treatment	A	B	C
Learning to cope with emotions, relationships, and daily life	A	B	C
Learning about and developing a plan to prevent relapse	A	B	C
Participating in activities that substitute for addiction	A	B	C

Stage 4 Experiences: Early Recovery and Rehabituation

Avoiding people, situations, and activities that trigger relapse	A	B	C
Developing behaviors that support health and social functioning	A	B	C
Restoring and building new relationships that support recovery	A	B	C
Engaging in activities that support recovery	A	B	C

Stage 5 Experiences: Active Recovery and Maintenance

Recalling daily the lessons learned from your addiction	A	B	C
Engaging in safe behaviors, activities, and relationships	A	B	C
Staying tuned to thoughts/feelings and remaining self-aware	A	B	C
Taking charge of and responsibility for your decisions	A	B	C

Getting Located

You've now been introduced to and thought about the stages of recovery. Your Checkpoint journal entry helped you identify where you are with respect to each of these stages. Now look at the Checkpoint answers you've circled, and complete the next entry.

WHERE ARE YOU?

1. Which four tasks are the most relevant to you *now*?

a. _____

b. _____

c. _____

d. _____

2. What do the tasks you picked tell you about your current level of recovery?

_____

_____

_____

_____

_____

3. What is your current stage in dealing with or understanding addiction?

___Stage 1   ___Stage 3   ___Stage 5

___Stage 2   ___Stage 4

4. Was it easy or difficult to identify your current stage? Why?

_____

_____

_____

_____

5. Do these "stages" fit your own particular experience of addiction? If they do, how? If not, how is your experience different?

_____

_____

_____

_____

6. What are your current goals for dealing with or better understanding this time in your life?

_____

_____

_____

_____

THINGS TO THINK ABOUT

- Does the idea that there are "stages" to recovery fit your own experience?
- Are you feeling encouraged by what you've read so far, or does the work ahead seem overwhelming?
- If you have a spouse or close family members, how are their needs and concerns affecting you and your decision-making process?

Using Your Feelings as a Guide

You now have a sense of your current stage, and whether you're even in recovery yet, as well as some of the tasks you face and those that are yet to come. But understanding the recovery continuum, and even being committed to the idea of recovery, doesn't make the process move any faster. Although you may make personal decisions about changing your behaviors and your life, the emotional and developmental issues of change evolve slowly over time. You can certainly influence (and even speed up) the process, but there are no shortcuts around the emotional issues and life situations that led to or have been caused by addiction and dependence.

Although you may make personal decisions about changing your behaviors and your life, the emotional and developmental issues of change evolve slowly over time.

There are many ways to tackle addiction and accomplish recovery. One goal of *The Healing Journey Through Addiction* is to help you think about and select your own route. Whichever route you choose, if it is to be successful it will be the result of a process of self-reflection.

This next journal entry will help you decide how best to use this book for yourself. It presents a checklist that can help you sort out your most pressing concerns and select those chapters that most fit your current needs.

IDENTIFYING YOUR CONCERNS

1. Check off all the items that best describe what you're generally feeling at this point in your life. (The numbers in parentheses next to each concern indicate the chapters most relevant to that concern.)

___afraid you can't overcome your addiction on your own (6, 8, 13)

___afraid you can't stop your addictive behaviors (2, 4, 6)

___afraid you'll lose your family, friends, job, or your life (4, 6, 13)

___angry at people who want you to change (2, 3, 4, 6)

___angry at yourself for your addiction (2, 4, 9)

___anxious about what your life will be like without your addiction (3, 4, 5, 14)

___ashamed of your behaviors or the problems that addiction has caused (5, 6, 9, 11)

___bitter about the events that contributed to your addiction (9, 10, 13)

___bitter about your family or friends (6, 11, 13, 15)

___confused about what to do or how to do it (2, 3, 4, 6)

___depressed about your life (9, 10, 12)

___desperate to stop (2, 3, 4, 6)

___detached from family, friends, people around you, and life (6, 10, 13, 15)

___frightened by your addiction (2, 3, 4, 6)

___guilty about your addiction (3, 4, 6, 12)

___helpless because you feel you can't stop (4, 6, 9, 12)

___lonely because your addiction has cut you off from other people (6, 13, 15) ___lost and don't know what to do (2, 3, 4, 6)

___numb and not feeling anything at all (6, 9, 14)

___overwhelmed by all you've been through (4, 6, 9, 10)

___overwhelmed by what's ahead (2, 6, 12)

___preoccupied with your addiction (2, 8, 14)

___resentful that you have to stop (2, 3, 4, 5, 11)

___sad about your life (3, 4, 6, 10)

___shocked by how people see you (4, 5, 11, 13)

___shocked by the idea that you have an addiction (2, 3, 4, 5)

___vulnerable and feeling exposed (6, 8, 13)

___worried about your future (2, 6, 10, 16)

___worried you won't be able to get and stay sober and clean (6, 7, 8)

___yearning for your addiction (5, 8)

2. Check off all the items that best describe those things you're doing or experiencing at this point in your life.

___avoiding family and friends? (5, 6, 11, 13)

___experiencing health problems? (3, 5, 14)

___failing or having difficulty in major life areas? (3, 4, 5, 6)

___hiding your behaviors? (3, 4, 5, 11)

___losing your temper when people approach you about your behaviors? (5, 6, 11)

___pretending things are okay when they're not? (3, 4, 9, 11)

___unable to avoid situations that keep you engaged in addictive behaviors? (8, 14)

___unable to cope with everyday life? (6, 8, 14)

___unable to deal with relationships? (6, 13)

___uncertain of what's important in your life? (4, 5, 13, 14)

___unsure of whether you really want to stop? (2, 3, 4, 5, 11)

3. Of the concerns you checked off in Question 1, which three are most intense right now?

a. _____

b. _____

c. _____

4. Of the experiences you checked off in Question 3, which three are most troubling right now?

a. _____

b. _____

c. _____

THINGS TO THINK ABOUT

- Do you share your feelings or experiences with anyone? If not, what stops you?
- Do your feelings seem so overwhelming at times that you need support?

Charting Your Own Course

By now, you have a clear sense of what addiction and dependence are, and what it means to enter and stay in recovery. What's immediately ahead is deciding if you *want* to proceed and how best to commit yourself to this journey of recovery and self-renewal. There will be bumps along the road, but if you use your journal you'll not only have a travel guide but also a companion on the road.

CHECKING IN WITH YOURSELF

1. *As I complete this chapter, I feel like . . .*

_____

_____

2. *Right now, I'd like to . . .*

_____

_____

3. *My most important current task is . . .*

_____

_____

4. *I feel like I most need to work on . . .*

_____

_____

5. *This time in my life is important because . . .*

_____

_____

THINGS TO THINK ABOUT

- Do you have a clear sense of the issues, feelings, and tasks you'll be facing?
- Are you asking your spouse, family members, and friends for their opinions, ideas, and support as you make decisions about your life?

3

Destination:

BEYOND DENIAL—AWAKENING

AND ACKNOWLEDGMENT

TRICIA

I started to get high in college and got involved in so many problem behaviors that I never really noticed they were problems until I failed every course one semester and came up before the college disciplinary committee. That was the first time I thought I might be a little out of control, but it took getting kicked out of school, two emergency room visits, three arrests, a bunch of abusive relationships, lost credit and big debt, and major problems with my family before I started to really sit up and pay attention.

Now I'm paying attention, but I still can't stop. I want to but I don't know how or where to begin. I just don't think I fit in with those self-help groups, and besides I can't see saying, "Hello, I'm Tricia and I'm an addict." Meantime, I'm still using. I could use some help right now.

ADDICTIVE BEHAVIORS ISOLATE you, and they make invisible the havoc they inflict: on you, those closest to you, and the world at large. People with addictions are blind. Luckily, you can use your family and friends as guides. What are your family and friends

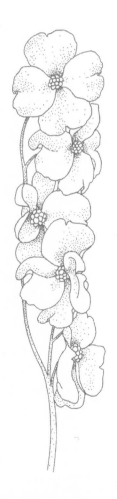

saying about your behaviors? Can you look around and check on the impact of your behaviors on your life and the lives of those closest to you?

This chapter is the first major step in your journey of recovery. Remember, in the words of the American poet Ralph Waldo Emerson, "the great majority of men are bundles of beginnings."

A Bundle of Addictions

The Healing Journey Through Addiction applies to all addictions. But not every addiction is the same. Some, such as drug addiction, involve behaviors that are illegal or socially unacceptable and must be kept hidden. Others involve behaviors that are legal but have limits to their social acceptability. Alcohol fits into this category. Some addictions, once illegal and considered immoral, are *big* business today and are promoted and encouraged, but they can easily get out of control. Alcohol (one of the biggest problems in the United States and other countries) and gambling are examples of addictions of this sort. When under their influence, these addictions can destroy both control and insight. Some addictions involve behavior that was once defined as normal and even desirable but is now viewed as socially unacceptable. The most obvious example is cigarettes. There are also addictions that are seen as normal, socially acceptable, and *benign,* such as coffee drinking. However, few people would argue that caffeine is not physically and emotionally addictive. The question remains as to what and how much damage is caused by caffeine and whether it will remain an acceptable addiction in the years to come. Addictions like this also beg the question of what threshold must be crossed, what damage must be caused, or what price paid before there is motivation for someone to want to quit the addiction.

Some addictions produce behavioral changes (alcohol), some produce mind-altering changes (alcohol and many drugs), some produce mood-altering and emotional changes (tranquilizers and drugs such as cocaine over time, as well as nicotine and caffeine), and some produce physical changes (food). These changes produced by addictive behavior can be dangerous to others (drunk driving) or to the addict (overeating). The changes can be rapid and immediately discernible or appear only over extended and continuous engagement in addictive behaviors. Sometimes they can go unnoticed; for instance, smokers and coffee drinkers don't usually behave differently after smoking a cigarette or having a cup of coffee. In these types of addictions, it's the *inability* to engage in the addiction that produces change. Many addictions produce several changes in several areas at the same time and over the long run. In the case of all addictions, however, the *absence* of the addiction produces change and the emotional and often physical discomfort and anxiety that helps to maintain and drive addiction. This is one of those hallmarks by which addiction can be most clearly identified.

What personal price or damage to health, relationships, social functioning, financial freedom, independence, or the lives of others must be paid before the addict decides to quit?

Why Quit?

Just as remaining addicted is a personal choice, so too is quitting the addiction. But why quit? What motivates the addict to give up the thing that brings relief? The realization that the relief is only temporary, that there is a price to pay for that relief, and that the price is too high is one motivating factor. However, for addictions that don't come with a high price, like caffeine use, quitting becomes more of a personal choice than a social, legal, or health imperative. For some addicts, no price is too high, and they die addicted, often because of their addiction.

So, what is the threshold? What personal price or damage to health, relationships, social functioning, financial freedom, independence, or the lives of others must be paid before the addict decides to quit? What is the threshold at which *you* will open your eyes and get beyond denying there's a problem? As you're reading this book, perhaps you've already reached or passed that point. Then again, perhaps someone gave you this book and you're reading it simply to get him or her off your back! This might be a good time for you to go back to Chapter 1 and review the first journal entry, How Did You Get This Book? Think about the decision you made about how you're going to use this book.

WHY QUIT?

1. Choose a word or a short phrase that describes what you think you may be addicted to. Repeat what you wrote the first time you completed this same question in Chapter 2 if you'd like, or take the opportunity to build on your last answer.

_____

_____

_____

2. *My addiction . . .*

___affects or bothers other people

___could result in danger to myself

___could result in danger to other people

___has effects that show up only over time

___has immediate or rapid effects

___is beyond my self control

___is illegal

other:_____

_____

_____

___is socially unacceptable

___must be kept hidden

___produces changes in my behavior

___produces changes in my health

___produces changes in the way I feel

___produces changes in the way I look

___produces changes in the way I think

_____

_____

_____

3. How do you feel about the effects you identified in Question 2?

_____

_____

_____

_____

4. Which effects concern you the most?

_____

_____

_____

_____

5. What must happen or what price must you pay to give up your addiction?

_____

_____

_____

_____

6. What price will your family or others important to you have to pay for you to give up your addiction?

_____

_____

_____

_____

7. What price will you have to pay if you don't give up your addiction?

_____

_____

_____

_____

8. What price will your family or others important to you have to pay if you don't give up your addiction?

_____

_____

_____

9. *My addiction . . .*

_____

_____

The Behaviors of Addiction

There are a number of "side" behaviors that often accompany addiction but are not part of the addiction per se. Addiction is so inherently antisocial—its main purpose is to feed itself with little regard for anyone or anything else—that it produces like behaviors needed to maintain the addiction.

Denial is a way to ignore or dismiss the idea of addiction and avoid seeing that there's a problem.

- *Denial.* Addicts often deny that there is an addiction. Perhaps the person is unaware that he or she is addicted, but more often the addict doesn't want to see or acknowledge the addiction. Denial is a way to ignore or dismiss the idea of addiction and avoid seeing that there's a problem. Sometimes addicts will acknowledge being addicted but dismiss the reality or significance of the addiction. Cigarette smoking is a good example of an addiction that people readily acknowledge but frequently do nothing about. They deny the reality of the addiction. Overcoming denial is always the first step in treatment of addictions.

- *Selfishness.* Addictions make people selfish because nothing is more important than the addiction itself. Everything is geared toward getting the dependence met, and the deeper into addiction the greater the selfishness. Addictions blind the addict.

- *Covert behavior.* Addictive behaviors often eventually become a source of concern for others and are seen as antisocial. To meet the obsessive and compulsive needs of the addiction, the addict often behaves illicitly, hiding the addictive behaviors from others, sneaking drugs, alcohol, cigarettes, food, or sex.

- *Irresponsibility and undependability.* In the throes of addiction, addicts must pay far more attention to the needs of their addiction than to the needs of anyone or anything else. They become increasingly unable to meet the social expectations and responsibilities of everyday life, whether in school, at work, or in relationships. They often cannot be counted on to fulfill their obligations to others.

- *Illegal and criminal behaviors.* There are some addictions in which even *engaging* in them is illegal. Sometimes the addict must commit criminal acts to get the desired substance or engage in the activity. Much street, computer, and white-collar crime is directed toward meeting the needs of addiction.

- *Dangerous and risky behaviors.* Because of the inherently antisocial and sometimes illegal or illicit nature of many addictions, addicts often must engage in dangerous behaviors to satisfy their needs. Slaves to the addiction, this may mean using a dirty needle, getting street drugs, going to an unsafe part of town, or interacting with dangerous people. Using the substance itself may be considered risky and dangerous. For example, cigarettes contain known carcinogens, and over-indulging in unhealthy foods can result in myriad physical health problems.

Although these sort of behaviors or consequences often accompany addiction, they are not always present. Some addicts are quite open about their addiction and do not even deny the possible consequences of it. They have chosen to pay the price (although not caring about the price may constitute a different form of denial).

In some cases, addicts learn to live with their addiction and find ways to met the needs of the addiction without having to give it up and enter treatment. Others retreat to a society composed of other addicts, thus choosing a lifestyle that supports their addiction. Depending on the social acceptability of the addiction, some addicts may have access to the desired object without having to sneak around or engage in illegal or dangerous activities; they can maintain their addictions openly.

Addicts who successfully live with their addiction represent only a small percentage of people addicted to a substance, object, or activity.

Addicts who successfully live with their addiction represent only a small percentage of people addicted to a substance, object, or activity. For most addicted people, the addiction eventually requires some form of underground behavior, and for many addicts keeping the addiction a secret is paramount, second in importance only to the addiction itself. Denial of the addiction is an important tool in the arsenal that keeps addiction alive.

Keeping Addictions Quiet

In the case of hidden addictions, many addicts try to have it both ways. They want to keep their addiction but have everyone think they've quit it. They think that their well-kept secret won't result in their having to pay a price. This is just another form of denial.

The first step to overcoming addiction is to get beyond denial. Using the Alcoholics Anonymous (AA) paradigm, to overcome an addiction you must first admit you are powerless over it and that your life has become unmanageable. Of course, you don't have to wait for your life to become unmanageable before you make a decision to enter recovery. In fact, it's preferable that you haven't allowed your addictive behaviors to take control of you, but however deep into your addiction you are, you must first recognize and acknowledge the problems that result from your addictive behaviors.

Use the next journal entry to think candidly about your behaviors. Being honest, even with ourselves, can be challenging and uncomfortable, under the best of circumstances. It can be even harder for addicts who have developed skills in deception (and self-deception) to maintain their addiction. Try hard to be honest as you work through this and all other journal entries. Remember, this is your journal and it need not be shared with anyone else unless you choose to share it.

BEYOND DENIAL

1. Look at each item in this self-evaluation of addictive behaviors and check off every item that applies to you:

___Do family members, friends, or other people express concern about your habit?

___Is your habit causing conflict with your spouse, family, or friends?

___Do you get angry with people who express concern about your habit?

___Do you hide your habit and behaviors from other people?

___Do you lie to other people so you can engage in your habit?

___Is indulging and engaging in your habit more important than your spouse, children, family, friends, or other people in your life?

___Are you paying more attention to your habit than you are to anyone or anything else?

___Do you ever engage in illegal activities to indulge your habit? Does your habit ever lead you to break the law? Is your habit itself illegal?

___Do you ever engage in dangerous or risky behaviors to satisfy the needs of your habit?

___Is your habit leading or contributing to problems with your physical health?

___Is your habit leading or contributing to problems with your mental health or emotional stability?

___Is your habit leading or contributing to problems in school or at work?

___Is your habit leading or contributing to problems in your relationships?

___Is your habit leading or contributing to financial problems?

___Is your habit leading or contributing to legal problems?

___Do you ever engage in your habit more than you planned or intended?

___Do you find yourself thinking about your habit, even when you're with other people?

___Do you find you need to engage more in your habit than you used to in order to feel the same high or sense of satisfaction?

___Have you ever tried to quit or cut back on your habit but found you can't?

___Do you feel depressed, guilty, or remorseful after you engage in your habit?

___Do you feel anticipation or relief just thinking about your habit?

___Are you afraid that you won't be able to function well if you quit your habit?

___Are you afraid you will lose your motivation or confidence if you quit your habit?

___Do you feel physical of emotional discomfort or a craving when your habit is unavailable or you go without engaging in the habit?

___No matter what anyone else says or how many problems your habit causes or contributes to, do you deny having an addiction?

2. Look at your answers. What do they tell you?

_____

_____

_____

_____

_____

_____

3. You've already looked at an Addiction Thermometer (Chapter 2). Now take a slightly different look. This time think strictly about how much your habits and addictive behaviors are affecting your life and your ability to function effectively and appropriately. On this continuum, *functional* means that your behaviors are not affecting your life in any significant way and that there are no significantly harmful consequences to your behaviors. *Dysfunctional* means that although you've managed to continue functioning and work around your behaviors, they are nevertheless having a significant impact on your ability to function well. *Nonfunctional* means that there is a serious disturbance in your ability to function at all in one or more areas of your life. Place a mark along the continuum that most approximates the impact of your habit on your ability to function effectively.

|---------------------------|---------------------------|
FUNCTIONAL   DYSFUNCTIONAL   NONFUNCTIONAL

4. Does your answer to Question 3 square with the evaluation you completed in Question 1? If not, why not? If it does, what does this tell you?

_____

_____

_____

_____

_____

_____

5. How does your answer to Question 3 fit with how you rated and described your level of functioning in Questions 1 to 5 of the Addiction Thermometer journal entry in Chapter 2? If it doesn't match, why is that? If it does, what does this tell you?

_____

_____

_____

_____

_____

6. Do other people worry about your habits or believe that you are addicted?

_____

_____

_____

_____

_____

7. Are you addicted? Explain.

_____

_____

_____

_____

_____

_____

THINGS TO THINK ABOUT

- Are these journal entries helping you to think about what it means to be addicted? Perhaps more important, are they helping you to understand what it means to be in recovery?
- Are you experiencing a habit, or is your "habit" really an addiction?
- Are you ready for recovery? Are you ready to *stay* with recovery?

Committing to the Process

As you near the end of this chapter, you are either learning you are not experiencing an addiction, you are moving closer to acknowledging an addiction, or you remain in denial (in which case you should read on for now but must later return to Chapter 2 and start working your way back through this book).

Although at this point you need not make a major commitment to abstinence or significantly moderating your addiction, it is time to consider committing yourself to the process of learning more about yourself, your behaviors, self-control, self-regulation, and journaling itself.

If you're serious about recovery, or at least learning more about it, you'll use *The Healing Journey Through Addiction* in the way intended. You'll treat every journal entry as an opportunity to write about your life and experiences and a means for exploring your thoughts, feelings, and behaviors. If used in this way, your recovery journal will represent a major investment of your time and energy and become a focal point for recovery, self-growth, and self-renewal. As in any relationship, you earn back only what you put in it.

Consider committing yourself to the process of learning more about yourself, your behaviors, self-control, self-regulation, and journaling itself.

Dead Ends and Side Roads

Remember those side roads and dead ends in this early stage of recovery: denial, dismissal, and disbelief. Alone or together, these ways of thinking will lead you away from recovery and back to active addiction. For anyone "habituated" into certain behaviors, it's easy to simply fall back into old patterns and ways of doing things.

One dead end is "thinking error." This is a way of thinking in which irrational ideas and beliefs shape our reality and the way we experience the world around us and become part of a self-defeating cycle. Simply put, negative thoughts shape your expectations and lead to ineffective and unsuccessful behaviors, which in turn lead to negative thoughts. For instance, if you think you're a failure you will always expect to fail. In this scenario, any rejection or lack of success is taken as confirmation that you are a failure and reinforces negative self-image. Just as success builds success, so does a sense of failure build a sense of failure. Thinking errors, or "cognitive distortions," are those negative ways of thinking that ensure failure.

Cognitive distortions can easily lead you away from recovery. In these early days of recovery it's important to identify and avoid cognitive distortions. This entry will help you learn to look for and recognize cognitive distortions.

BEWARE OF DENIAL

1. Check off any of the following cognitive distortions that apply to the way you think.

___After all that happened yesterday, I deserve to [your addictive behavior here].

___After all that's happened lately, I really could use [your addictive behavior here].

___After all that's happened lately, I really need [your addictive behavior here].

___Everyone else is [your addictive behavior here]. I'll seem weird if I don't as well.

___I can stop if I want to. I just don't want to.

___I can't get through today without [your addictive behavior here].

___I haven't [your addictive behavior here] for a week now. That shows I'm not addicted.

___I'm really going through a difficult time and need [your addictive behavior here].

___I really don't have a problem and can afford to indulge in [your addictive behavior here].

___I've done so well that I deserve to [your addictive behavior here].

___Just one [your addictive behavior here] won't hurt.

___No one will even notice if I [your addictive behavior here].

___Things at work/school are especially tough right now. I just need [your addictive behavior here] to get through this temporary period.

___Today's a special occasion. I'm entitled to [your addictive behavior here].

___What's the big deal anyway if I [your addictive behavior here]?

___What the hell. I can always stop [your addictive behavior here] some other time.

2. Describe three other cognitive distortions (or rationalizations for engaging in your addiction) that you have actually been experiencing or can think of.

a. _____

b. _____

c. _____

3. Are you prepared to believe your cognitive distortions? Explain.

_____

_____

_____

_____

4. Are you willing to slip back into denial? Explain.

_____

_____

_____

_____

_____

THINGS TO THINK ABOUT

- Do cognitive distortions, errors in thinking, and rationalizations help maintain your addiction?
- Do thinking errors influence or shape other aspects of your life? If so, how?
- Is it important to recognize and correct errors in thinking?

Getting in Touch With Yourself:
The Ninety-Second Notebook

Changing behaviors is terribly difficult. It takes not only commitment but a great deal of time and work. Old, established behaviors must be replaced with new, healthy behaviors.

Do not feel ashamed of the things you are writing in your notebook. . . . Write about your feelings, but don't be self-critical.

The last entry in this chapter runs over twenty-one consecutive days. You'll have to buy a small notebook and keep that pad and a pen with you throughout each day. Each time a thought or feeling about your addiction pops into your mind, or each time you engage in your addiction, take ninety seconds out of your day to write down the thought, feeling, craving, or experience. Working on this entry will keep you focused on yourself and allow you to really start thinking about just how often addiction pops up in your daily world. As you write each ninety-second note, follow these simple rules:

- If a day goes by without writing, extend the twenty-one days by one day. Do not berate yourself, call yourself a failure, or give up because you can't do it.

- Do not feel ashamed of things you are writing in your notebook. Shame feeds addictions; it does not stop them. The more accurate and honest your notebook is, the more helpful it will be to you.

- In your notebook write about your feelings, but don't be self-critical. That is, you can write "I feel so stupid to have smoked a cigarette without thinking about what I was doing" because that may be an honest report of your feelings. You cannot write "What a stupid idiot I was to smoke a cigarette without thinking about it" because that is being self-critical.

- If you slip and make a self-critical statement in your notebook, don't feel guilty or berate yourself. Simply circle it in red, draw a small arrow pointing toward it, and label it "self-critical statement." Addicts are often self-critical, so don't expect to avoid such statements in your notebook. The goal is simply to make fewer and fewer as the twenty-one days go on.

- Don't cross out, rip out, or throw out things you write. You wrote them for a reason, even if they later upset you or you disagree with them. Everything you write in the notebook is in some way a part of you, and a crucial part of dealing with addictions is learning to recognize and accept ourselves, with our strengths and our flaws.

For each of the twenty-one days, take just ninety seconds at a time to record:

- *Your thoughts and feelings about your addiction.* These can include how addiction affects your life or the lives of others, and what the costs of addiction are to you.

- *Each craving or need to indulge your addiction and the triggers, situations, or memories that led to the feeling.* Understanding the triggers that set off a craving is a critical part of any plan to prevent relapse.

- *Your experience any time you give in to an impulse and indulge your addiction.* Keeping a daily record of when you engage in your addictive behaviors is a crucial part of recovery. Record what you did, what the effects were, and what led to your decision to engage.

Keeping a daily record of when you engage in your addictive behaviors is a crucial part of recovery.

- *Ideas and information about your addiction.* Keep track of the things you're learning about your addiction: its occurrence among other people, its ill effects, and so on. These may be things you hear on the radio or TV, read in the newspaper, hear from a friend, or read in a book about your addiction.

- *What's available to help people with your addiction.* Make note of phone numbers and hot lines, self-help groups, treatment programs, workbooks, therapists, or addiction counselors.

◆ *Other people's reactions to your addiction.* Do other people comment on it? Do they say things that make you angry?

At the end of each day, summarize the day's worth of notes from your ninety-second notebook in the next entry, and do this for each of the twenty-one days.

A NINETY-SECOND NOTEBOOK

"Great things are not done by impulse, but
by a series of small things brought together."
—VINCENT VAN GOGH

Day: _____   Date: _____   Day No.: _____

1. Summarize up to ten of the ninety-second notes you wrote to yourself. If you wrote more than ten, pick the most significant. You'll need the entry blank for repeated use.

a. _____

b. _____

c. _____

d. _____

e. _____

f. _____

g. _____

h. _____

i. _____

j. _____

2. What best describes the overall theme of your ninety-second notebook for today?

_____

_____

_____

3. Reflect on what you've learned from today's ninety-second notebook.

_____

_____

_____

4. If this is Day 2 or beyond of this entry, are you learning more about yourself and your addictive behaviors each day? If so, what are you learning?

_____

_____

_____

5. Is there an idea or a goal you want to focus your attention on for tomorrow's ninety-second notebook?

_____

_____

_____

6. If this is the last day of the twenty-one-day process, what have you learned and where are you heading?

_____

_____

_____

_____

THINGS TO THINK ABOUT

- Did your ninety-second notebook help you to stay in touch with your ideas, thoughts, feelings, cravings, and experiences throughout the day?
- Did you make at least ten ninety-second entries today? If not, why not, and what does this mean?
- Is it difficult to maintain this sort of focus? Are you committed to working this hard during this early part of recovery?

4

Destination:
UNDERSTANDING YOUR
ADDICTION

JACKSON

*I really convinced myself I wasn't addicted. I was one of those classic
people who could stop if I wanted to; I just didn't want to. I had all
sorts of explanations for my behavior, and they were all really
pretty convenient. They allowed me to avoid having to take anyone
seriously when they approached me about what they saw as my
problem, and they also allowed me to give 101 reasons for why I behaved that way, and none of them included addiction. I knew what
an addiction was, and I didn't have one.*

*But somewhere in the back of my head (or maybe in the back of
my heart) I knew I had a problem. In fact, somewhere back there I
knew I couldn't stop even if I wanted to. I knew I'd lost jobs, friends,
and girlfriends because of my addiction but just didn't want to
admit it. But my eyes started to open after I got into a new relationship (that I really wanted to work out) with someone whose mother
had an addiction and had died. I started to look out how my behaviors had damaged and were in the process of ruining my life. I began
to see things I'd managed to not see before and figured it was finally*

time to admit the truth and do something about it and start going through life with eyes wide open instead of wide shut.

WHAT REMAINS IN the early awareness and acknowledgment stage of addiction is fully *understanding* its meaning and impact in your life. Giving up an addiction means giving up something that has played a significant role in your life and added meaning to it. It's not easy to give this up, but better understanding it will help you enter recovery and stay there.

This chapter marks the bridge from Stage 1 to Stage 2—from a stage of prerecovery to an early stage of actual recovery. You will more fully understand addiction and how your own behaviors fit into a pattern of addiction.

You've already written a few brief words about your addiction and what you think you may be addicted to. The next journal entry will help you continue this exploration.

Giving up an addiction means giving up something that has played a significant role in your life and added meaning to it.

MY ADDICTION

1. Name your addiction.

_____

_____

2. Describe your addiction by completing these sentences.

a. *My addiction is . . .* _____

_____

b. *My addiction makes me . . .* _____

_____

c. *My addiction makes me feel . . .* _____

_____

d. *When I'm using or engaged in my addiction I . . .* _____

_____

e. *I love my addiction because* . . . _____

_____

f. *I hate my addiction because* . . . _____

_____

3. When did you first begin to engage in these addictive behaviors?

_____

_____

_____

_____

4. When did you first start to think you had a problem with these behaviors?

_____

_____

_____

_____

5. When did you first start to think you had an addiction?

_____

_____

_____

6. When did you first start to think you should do something about this problem?

_____

_____

_____

7. Write a sentence that includes in it the addiction you've described as your own.

_____

_____

_____

_____

8. How does the sentence you just wrote compare with your previous sentences in Chapters 2 and 3?

_____

_____

_____

_____

9. Is your thinking about your addiction changing?

_____

_____

_____

_____

THINGS TO THINK ABOUT

- Was this a difficult journal entry? Were you able to describe why you love and hate your addiction? Are these journal entries making sense to you, or are you just going through the steps of completing them?
- Is your journal having any impact on your thinking or your behaviors? If not, why not?
- Are you sharing your experiences with this journal with anyone else? If so, is it useful? If not, what stops you?

The Stuff of Addiction

We live in a society filled with the "stuff" of addiction. It is the nature of advertising and the media to inundate us with images that tempt and entice, but these glamorous representations of alcohol, tobacco, food, medications, sex, and gambling can become a source of anxiety and provide potent triggers for relapse.

Although addiction is a personal responsibility, our society has a role in marketing it. During the next twenty-four hours, pay close attention to how the stuff of addiction is packaged and sold to you. In particular, take note of the following:

- advertising (magazine, newspaper, billboard, television, and radio)
- the content of current movies and television shows of every kind
- music and music videos
- radio disc jockeys and talk-show hosts
- popular-magazine articles
- the fashion world
- the Internet

Use the next journal entry to record your findings.

It is the nature of advertising and the media to inundate us with images that tempt and entice, but these glamorous representations of alcohol, tobacco, food, medications, sex, and gambling can become a source of anxiety and provide potent triggers for relapse.

MONITORING THE MEDIA

1. What did you learn from watching and listening to the media?

_____

_____

_____

_____

2. What did you learn about the way the media shape or influence the way people respond to the "stuff" of addictions?

_____

_____

_____

_____

3. What did you learn about the way media advertise, disseminate information, and treat the things that make up *your* addiction?

_____

_____

_____

_____

_____

4. Do the media oppose your addiction, or do they in some way condone and support it?

_____

_____

_____

_____

_____

5. How do the media affect or tempt your addiction?

_____

_____

_____

_____

_____

6. How can you best deal with the media messages and images that tempt your addiction?

_____

_____

_____

_____

_____

- Did you find that your addiction is or has been influenced and affected by the media? If so, are the media responsible for your addiction, or are you?
- Why isn't everyone more affected by media messages that promote the stuff of addictions?
- Do you need to find ways to avoid messages that promote, condone, or in some other way tempt and influence your addiction?

The Role of Addiction

There are many different ideas and theories about why some people become addicted and others don't and what happens to a person once addicted. Regardless of how they're acquired, addictions are more than just personal choices or disease, the result of social environment or genetics. Addictions serve a *purpose* of some kind. This is the "other" side of addiction.

There are those who believe it doesn't matter why or how an addiction is acquired. Their only concern is that an addiction exists and must be eliminated. From this point of view, insight into the source of the addiction is unnecessary. But to understand and eliminate an addiction without fully understanding it is risky if the addiction *also* serves a purpose that remains unfilled once the addiction is gone. In other words, addictions often substitute for something missing from the emotional life of the addict. Without the addiction, that emotional hole will remain waiting to be filled. Accordingly, unless something positive and emotionally rewarding fills that void, the addiction will simply reappear to fill the hole once again or be replaced by another addiction.

In many ways, self-help organizations such as AA serve as the substitute for the addiction, thus filling the emotional gap that's left. The organization's philosophy, meetings, and structure, as well

Something must take the place of addiction if recovery is to be successful in the long run.

as the personal relationships that are formed via these meetings, take the place of the addiction. For this reason, it's considered important to continue attending AA meetings for many years after entering recovery. Other self-help organizations, however, oppose this sort of substitution, believing that AA-style groups (as well as substance-abuse counseling in general) simply replace the addiction and never allow former addicts to stand on their own two feet. *Something* must take the place of addiction if recovery is to be successful in the long run, but in the end it will be up to you to decide which direction to take.

Use the next journal entry to think about the roles that addiction plays in your life and the ways in which it is important. This may seem like a way to convince yourself to stay addicted, but in reality to replace addiction you first must understand the function it plays in your life.

DYSFUNCTIONAL FUNCTIONS

1. *My addiction . . .*

___adds excitement to my life

___allows me to be myself

___allows me to say what I really want to say

___allows me to see things clearly

___allows me to tolerate all the other stuff in my life

___allows me to tolerate people and things I couldn't otherwise stand

___gives me a different view of the world

___gives me a sense of control

___gives me a sense of freedom

___gives me confidence

___gives me courage

___gives me something to look forward to

___helps me feel less depressed

___helps me fit in

___helps me forget my troubles

___improves my life

___improves my sex life

___keeps people away

___makes me feel better   ___makes me less shy

___makes me feel better about myself   ___makes me more attractive

___makes me feel numb   ___makes me more creative

___makes me forget about the world   ___makes me more outgoing

___makes me less inhibited   ___provides a way to avoid difficulties

other: _____   _____

_____   _____

_____   _____

2. List five reasons to stay addicted.

_____

_____

_____

_____

_____

3. What are the advantages of addiction?

_____

_____

_____

4. How does addiction help you to live your life?

_____

_____

_____

5. What is the *primary* role that addiction plays in your life?

_____

_____

_____

6. What's missing from your life that makes addiction so important?

_____

_____

_____

_____

_____

THINGS TO THINK ABOUT

- Was it difficult or easy to understand the role(s) played by addiction in your life and the advantages to staying addicted? Was working on this entry depressing or empowering?
- Did this entry help you to develop more insight into your addiction? Do you want to give up your addiction?
- Was it difficult to answer Question 6?

Routines, Rituals, and Addiction

Positive rituals enhance and give meaning to our lives and relationships, but negative ones perpetuate self-defeating and antisocial behaviors.

Our lives are made up of schedules, routines, and rituals. Schedules help us to stick to our routines, but rituals give *meaning* to our schedules and routines. Rituals help maintain our connection with others, our sense of identity, and even our health. They encompass family relationships and interactions; religious and spiritual life; seasonal holidays and festivities; and daily activities such as exercise, relaxation, and family meals. Rituals define not just what we do but also how and when we do it.

Rituals can be positive or negative. Positive rituals enhance and give meaning to our lives and relationships, but negative ones perpetuate self-defeating and antisocial behaviors. A glass of wine with dinner may enhance a special meal, or it may be the first of several glasses drunk to ease the stress from a day at work. The latter illustrates a negative ritual that's part of a self-destructive cycle. Drinking becomes an addictive ritual rather than a relaxation ritual.

Use the next journal entry to think about how your addiction has affected positive rituals in your life and how you've built negative rituals around your addiction.

OBSERVANCES AND PRACTICES

1. Name six rituals or routines in your life that are important to you:

a. _____ d. _____

b. _____ e. _____

c. _____ f. _____

2. In what ways has your addiction generally affected or disrupted these rituals?

_____

_____

_____

_____

_____

3. Pick one ritual that has clearly been affected or disrupted at least once. Describe how your addiction affected the ritual.

_____

_____

_____

_____

_____

_____

4. Who was most affected by the disruption caused by your addiction?

_____

_____

_____

_____

5. What new rituals have you developed that support your addiction?

_____

_____

_____

_____

6. Are the rituals that support your addiction positive (and harmless) or negative (and self-destructive)?

_____

_____

_____

7. If you answered "positive" to Question 6, in what ways are your addiction rituals positive? How do they contribute meaningfully to your life, relationships, or health? If your answer was "negative," in what ways are your addiction rituals negative? How do they take away from your life, relationships, or health?

_____

_____

_____

_____

8. Do you need to develop, rebuild, or return to positive rituals in your life?

_____

_____

_____

- Were you able to identify important rituals in your life? If not, why not? If so, is there any pattern to these rituals?
- Are your main observances related more to your addiction than to your spirituality, relationships, health, or ability to function well?
- If you answered "positive" to Question 6, are you fooling yourself? What might others say? Would you consider asking others what they think?

Checking in on Commitment

As you reach the end of this chapter, you should have a greater understanding not only of your addiction but also of the role it plays in your life and how your life is shaped by your addiction. Try to assess your commitment to recovery at this point in time. Recovery entails:

- resolution of issues
- stability in terms of daily, weekly functioning
- sanity and clear thinking
- consistency in the short and long run
- reliability, dependability, and predictability
- capacity to cope, manage, grow
- restoration and resumption of relationships, health, and life

Are you ready for recovery? What does recovery mean to you at this point? Can you recover without giving up your addiction? Use the final journal entry in this chapter to reflect on your work, your thoughts, and your interest in recovery so far.

CHECKPOINT: RECOVERY

1. What have you learned about your addiction?

_____

_____

_____

_____

_____

2. Complete these sentences to describe what recovery means to you at this point.

a. *For me, recovery means . . .* _____

_____

b. *Being recovered means . . .* _____

_____

3. Are you ready to commit to abstinence or to modifying addictive behaviors?

_____

_____

_____

THINGS TO THINK ABOUT

- Are you ready to enter or stay with recovery? Are you ready to begin Chapter 5, or should you work through Chapters 2 through 4 again?
- Are you sharing your experiences, thoughts, or feelings with anyone else? If not, why not? If so, is sharing providing help and support, and encouragement?
- Have you taken any of those Stage 1 dead ends or side roads: denial, dismissal, or disbelief?

5

Destination:

THE PRESENT—

THE PRICE YOU PAY

"Thou source of all my
bliss and all my woe,
That found'st me poor
at first, and keep'st
me so."
—OLIVER GOLDSMITH

LINDSEY

What a price I've paid for being an addict. I've been in detox, hospitals, and rehab over forty times. Even though I'm a skilled secretary, I haven't been able to hold down a job for more than a few days. I've lost two marriages, and none of my grown children want anything to do with me. I live off welfare, depend on detox or rehab just for housing, and I have no health to speak of. All my friends (if you can call them that) are addicts also, and every romantic relationship (if you can call them that) are with people who need to get high as much (or more) than they need me. I don't have a life. The worst part is I know it, but I still can't stop. Sometimes I want to, but most of the time I don't even care.

TOM

My weight has been a problem for over twenty years. I wasn't always this way, but over the years my compulsion to eat got completely away from me. My wife stayed with me at first but finally wanted out of the relationship, and left. My kids were a mixed

bag, and my youngest was actually quite cruel to me with his constant comments about my weight and the way I look. I've never lost a job because of my weight, but I know I haven't been able to get new jobs or a promotion because of it. I can't walk without effort, and my health is shot. My addiction for food long ago took over my life.

Recovery is a process that requires a great deal of commitment and support, but above all you need to get beyond denial.

IF YOU'VE BEEN working sequentially through *The Healing Journey Through Addiction,* by this point you're in the active stage of recovery. This second stage is a period of consideration and incubation during which you're considering the costs of continuing addiction, the benefits of recovery, the work involved; you're also moving toward some significant decisions. If you successfully accomplish the tasks of this stage, you will have decided that recovery is the life you want, free of addiction.

The tasks of this stage include listening to others, considering the consequences of your addiction to yourself and others, recognizing that addiction is not moving your life in a positive direction, and thinking about what can happen if you overcome your addiction. If you're not ready to tackle these tasks and change the way you look at, listen to, and interact with the world, then you're not ready for the work in this chapter and are advised to continue working in the prerecovery chapters. Recovery is a process that requires a great deal of commitment and support, but above all you need to get beyond denial.

The Past, Present, and Future

Addiction has a history, present and future. In later chapters you'll have the opportunity to think back on the roots of and future course for your addiction, but the focus of this chapter is the present—your addiction in your life *today.*

To assess its impact, all you need to do is look. But you must look with open eyes and mind and be willing to accept the truth without extraneous rationalizations.

Use the next journal entry to explore what your addiction has cost you and those around you.

THE COSTS OF ADDICTION

1. How has addiction affected your life? Check off every item that applies, and add others below.

__accidents	__loss of important relationships
__bankruptcy	__loss of job or school
__damage to my reputation	__loss of opportunities
__damage to my self-esteem	__lost or damaged friendships
__financial problems	__lost or damaged important relationships
__hospitalizations or rehab	__lost or damaged marriage
__injury to others	__lost or damaged physical fitness
__jail	__lost or damaged romantic relationships
__legal problems	__mental health problems
__loss of children	__physical health problems
__loss of home	__traffic accidents

other: _____   _____

_____   _____

_____   _____

_____   _____

_____   _____

2. Who else is affected by your addiction? Check off anyone who's been affected, and briefly describe the effect of your addiction on each of these people. Add more below.

	How does your addiction affect
Who	*this person/these people?*
___spouse/partner	_____
___children	_____
___parents	_____
___friends	_____
___work colleagues	_____
___siblings	_____
___neighbors	_____
___community members	_____
___innocent bystanders	_____
other: _____	_____
_____	_____
_____	_____
_____	_____
_____	_____

3. *Addiction has made me . . .*

___callous and uncaring   ___a poor friend

___a criminal   ___a poor parent

___dangerous to others   ___a poor spouse/partner

___harmful to others   ___someone that people avoid

___irresponsible   ___unattractive to others

___lose interest in people or things   ___unreliable

___lose sight of what's important   ___untrustworthy

other: _____   _____

_____   _____

_____   _____

_____   _____

4. *People see me as . . .*

__a failure   __someone to feel sorry for

__an outcast   __unreliable

__incapable   __untrustworthy

__someone to be avoided   __weak

other: _____   _____

_____   _____

_____   _____

_____   _____

5. Are there any positive consequences or outcomes of your addiction?

_____

_____

_____

_____

_____

THINGS TO THINK ABOUT

- Was this a difficult journal entry? If it wasn't, why not? If it was, what was the most difficult part of it?
- Was it difficult to be honest? Was it difficult to look at the consequences of addiction with such negative eyes?
- Were you able to come up with any positive consequences of your addiction? If you were, are they *really* positive?

Realizing the Costs of Your Addiction

Addiction strips you raw. Use the next journal entry to think about the losses you've faced and had to accept because of your addiction.

AN INVENTORY OF LOSSES

1. What opportunities have you lost because of your addiction?

_____

_____

_____

_____

2. What relationships have been missed, damaged, or lost because of your addiction?

_____

_____

_____

_____

3. What experiences have you missed out on because of your addiction?

_____

_____

_____

_____

4. Summarize in a list everything you've lost or lost out on because of your addiction. Continue your list on a separate piece of paper, if necessary.

a. _____ d. _____

b. _____ e. _____

c. _____ f. _____

g. _____   i. _____

h. _____   j. _____

5. If you *weren't* addicted, what might be different?

_____

_____

_____

_____

6. Complete these sentences.

a. *If I weren't addicted, my life* . . . _____

_____

b. *If I weren't addicted, I would* . . . _____

_____

c. *If I weren't addicted, I could* . . . _____

_____

d. *If I weren't addicted, I would never have lost* . . . _____

_____

e. *If I weren't addicted, life would be* . . . _____

_____

7. What might you have given to your family and friends if you weren't addicted?

_____

_____

_____

8. What might you have received from family and friends if you weren't addicted?

_____

_____

_____

- Are these journal entries helping you make decisions about recovery, or are you finding them difficult to deal with? If working on them is difficult, are you getting the help you may need to work through them successfully?
- Is this recovery journey moving too fast for you, or is the pace manageable?
- Do you feel hopeful that losses can be reversed if you can overcome addiction?

Enabling the Addiction

Whether they mean to or not, sometimes people who support your recovery and who want you to quit your addiction may behave in ways that allow your addiction to continue. This behavior is known as enabling.

Whether they mean to or not, sometimes people who support your recovery and who want you to quit your addiction may behave in ways that allow your addiction to continue. This behavior is known as enabling. People enable, support, and encourage addiction in many ways.

- They *ignore* the addictive behaviors as though they weren't happening.
- They *encourage* the addiction, for instance, by inviting the alcoholic to drink with them.
- They *tempt* the addiction by engaging in the behavior themselves, such as eating rich foods in front of the eating addict or smoking in front of the nicotine addict.
- They *protect* the addict from any consequences of his or her behavior by paying bills, providing excuses, and so on. Their taking responsibility for the addict thus takes responsibility away from the addict.
- They *excuse* the addict, helping to fabricate reasons that rationalize addictive behavior and its consequences.
- They *forgive* the addict for any and all wrong doings, absolving him or her of any personal responsibility.

- They *fear* the consequences of confronting the addict.
- They *pretend* all is well, when it isn't.

By supporting the addiction, family and friends also become part of the denial or silence that surrounds addiction.

Benefiting from Addiction

Some enablers may benefit from someone else's addiction. Children, for example, may realize they can push the limits more easily with a less-attentive, alcoholic parent. A husband may be accustomed to having a vulnerable wife and may even feel threatened by her renewed self-esteem that comes with recovery. Therefore it is not just the addict's behavior patterns that must change but also those of the "supportive" enabler.

Use the next entry to think about who may be enabling your addiction or in some way benefiting from it. The entry focuses on a single person only, so use it repeatedly to think about each person on the list you'll create for the entry.

It is not just the addict's behavior patterns that must change but also those of the "supportive" enabler.

ENABLERS

1. In the first journal entry of this chapter, The Costs of Addiction, you created a list of people affected by your addiction. Now create a new list that includes family members, romantic interests, friends, coworkers, people you supervise, neighbors, and so on who are both affected by your addiction and somehow enable, maintain, support, allow, or benefit from it. Check off all areas that apply.

2. Name of Person Who . . .	Enables	Maintains	Supports	Allows	Benefits
_____	—	—	—	—	—
_____	—	—	—	—	—
_____	—	—	—	—	—
_____	—	—	—	—	—

Name of Person Who . . .	Enables	Maintains	Supports	Allows	Benefits
_____	—	—	—	—	—
_____	—	—	—	—	—
_____	—	—	—	—	—
_____	—	—	—	—	—
_____	—	—	—	—	—
_____	—	—	—	—	—
_____	—	—	—	—	—
_____	—	—	—	—	—

3. For the remainder of this entry, focus on just one person on this list.

Person: _____ (Repeat the entry for every person on your list.)

4. Check off all the ways this person affects your addiction.

___ enables   ___ maintains   ___ supports   ___ allows   ___ benefits

5. In what way does this person enable or benefit from your addiction?

_____

_____

_____

_____

_____

6. What must/could you do to change this person's behavior so that it enables you to enter recovery rather than remain addicted?

_____

_____

_____

_____

_____

7. What have you learned about enabling?

_____

_____

_____

_____

8. What have you learned about the way that your addiction benefits other people?

_____

_____

_____

_____

9. What will you do with these new ideas?

_____

_____

_____

_____

THINGS TO THINK ABOUT

- Are people in your support system helping you *stay* addicted?
- Some people who want to support your recovery may not know how to address issues with you. Do *you* know how to address issues with them?

A Picture of Your Addiction

To complete the next journal entry, turn to magazines, photographs, newspaper headlines, advertisements, drawings, artwork, and anything else that somehow captures or reflects your life as it was or as it has become.

Create a collage from these words and images that represents the effect and impact that addiction has had on your life and the lives of others. Use as the organizing theme the *price* of addiction. Because collages are made up of *found* words, pictures, and objects, not your own, they provide an opportunity for you to think about your world through other people's ideas and your reorganizing of their ideas.

A PICTURE OF ADDICTION

1. Create a collage, using the space provided on page 89 or on a separate sheet of paper.

2. How does this collage represent the costs of addiction in your life?

_____

_____

_____

_____

_____

3. If you described this collage to someone without sight, what would you say?

_____

_____

_____

_____

4. How did you feel as you were creating the collage?

_____

_____

_____

_____

_____

CREATE YOUR COLLAGE IN THIS SPACE

5. How do you feel when you look at it now?

_____

_____

_____

_____

6. What have you learned about your addiction from this collage?

_____

_____

_____

_____

7. Give your collage a title. _____

THINGS TO THINK ABOUT

- Would you consider mounting and framing this collage so that you can look at it every day? Would seeing it remind you of the costs of your addiction?
- Can you show this collage to other people in your life? If not, why not?

If this wasn't a difficult chapter, then you're not addicted, still in denial, untouched by the tragedy of your addiction, or unusually adept at bravely facing up to the realities of your life.

Picturing Your Life

How are you feeling as you complete this chapter? This should have been a difficult chapter because facing addiction is a painful process. If this wasn't a difficult chapter, then you're not addicted, still in denial, untouched by the tragedy of your addiction, or unusually adept at bravely facing up to the realities of your life.

This chapter's final journal entry will provide an opportunity for you to think about and express your thoughts and feelings and to assess your stage along this journey and your ability and willingness to keep traveling.

HOW MANAGEABLE IS YOUR LIFE?

1. How do you feel as you complete this chapter?

_____

_____

_____

_____

_____

2. What's the most difficult aspect of this work so far?

_____

_____

_____

_____

_____

3. Review Chapter 2, and think about the different stages of recovery again. Based on the work you've done so far, what recovery stage are you currently in?

___ Stage 1: Awareness/   ___ Stage 4: Early Recovery/
      Early Acknowledgment   Rehabituation

___ Stage 2: Consideration/Incubation   ___ Stage 5: Active Recovery/Maintenance

___ Stage 3: Exploring Recovery/
      Early Activity

4. This statement is paraphrased from the AA twelve-step recovery model (and is a basic tenet of similar self-help groups too): We admitted we were powerless over our addiction and that our lives had become unmanageable. Is this statement true for you?

_____

_____

_____

_____

5. How committed are you to recovery right now?

_____

_____

_____

_____

_____

_____

_____

_____

THINGS TO THINK ABOUT

- Are you ready for recovery? Are you ambivalent? Do you need to go back and do more work before moving on, or are you ready to continue on this journey?
- Is recovery moving too slowly for you? Is it moving too fast? How easily did you think recovery would come?
- Do you think recovery is something you can do alone, or do you think you need a powerful support system of friends and family to help? Is your current support system aware of all the issues you're thinking about at this stage of your journey and all that you're going through?

6

Destination:
GETTING SUPPORT

MARTIN

I couldn't have gotten over my alcoholism on my own. I must've quit a dozen times, sometimes for months at a time, but I always went back. In the end, it wasn't the groups I went to (and still do), the counseling, or the detox that worked. It was my accepting the help. I finally got over my lousy attitude of expecting others to do the work for me and somehow making me better. It was my accepting that I needed help in many areas of my life, and not just one or two. And once I accepted that I began to see and use help differently. I couldn't have done it alone and have had many friends and supporters to thank for helping me make the changes in my life I needed to make.

AMY

It took me years to learn about help. I either pretended I didn't need it, turned it down, didn't use it, or looked for it in all the wrong places. Sometimes I even blamed the help I got for my problems, as though my problems were the result of poor help. In one way or another it was as though the tools for self-help were there, but I didn't know how to use them. When I finally learned to get the right kind of help and committed myself to working with my helpers (and not against them), I found the strength to use the help and get on with my life.

THERE ARE MANY people who give up their addiction without joining a self-help group, seeking individual or group therapy, or entering a treatment program (indeed, there are self-help organizations that believe it's imperative for the addict to learn the skills of recovery *without* falling back on organized meetings or depending on treatment). However, many more helping professionals and organizations made up of recovering (and recovered) addicts *do* feel that help, in some form or another, is imperative.

The provision of support, guidance, instruction, and help is the cornerstone of all communities, whether religious, familial, or tribal.

The provision of support, guidance, instruction, and help is the cornerstone of all communities, whether religious, familial, or tribal. Although there may be individuals capable of overcoming their addiction without any support at all, support *will* make the road easier to travel, and for many without support there can be no recovery.

This chapter asks you to take a stand. Are you ready to enter recovery and commit yourself to it, or will you meander back down a side road and off into addiction? First, you'll need to think about what it means to get help and determine what sort of help is available to you.

Systems of Support

There are many kinds of support systems.

1. A *passive* support system provides you with the ear, the sympathy, and the emotional support of friends or family members. The support is passive because it has no tangible consequences. It doesn't pay the bills, it doesn't provide immediate

answers, it doesn't remove the source of the problem, and it doesn't reduce your need to eventually confront and tackle the problem face on. This type of support is enormously important, though, and it fits many needs: it allows you to unload your feelings and thus share your emotional burden, it provides encouragement and reassurance, and it fills the spiritual need of being connected to something else. In some ways this may be the most critical form of support. It's the glue that keeps us together.

2. A *practical* support system is one in which a helper offers very concrete and tangible assistance. This can range from financial loans, to physical help, taking care of the kids, providing meaningful advice, and pointing you in the right direction.

3. An *affiliative* system of support comprises family and friends who stand by but perhaps don't know what you're going through and others who may be new in your life but know exactly what you're going through because they've been through it themselves. Included in this category is a *professional* support system available from mental health and addiction counselors, health care providers, and other specialists who have had training and experience helping in situations very much like your own.

4. Finally, you have both a *natural* support system available to you as well as a *drafted,* or recruited, support system. Natural support includes the sort of help provided by family, friends, and others in your life who see your troubles for themselves; drafted support requires you (or someone acting on your behalf) to go out and get the support. Natural supporters are already in your circle of support, but drafted supporters must be sought out.

For most people, an effective support system is made up of a *web* of different kinds of support, which meet different needs at

An effective support system is made up of a web of different kinds of support, which meet different needs at different times and under different circumstances.

different times and under different circumstances. Many of these support systems overlap. A friend who provides emotional help can also provide practical support; a drafted supporter also becomes a provider of emotional support; and a professional supporter, such as an addiction counselor, can also provide affiliative support because he or she may be a recovering addict.

Damaged Support Systems

Often, people with serious addictions have damaged or failed to maintain their support system, or they have an inadequate system that cannot meet all their needs.

For instance, many addicts have lost the passive and emotional help offered by family and friends because of the damage the addictive behavior has caused to their relationships. Perhaps the cost of supporting the addiction has left them without money to pay for professional support. In some cases, the denial required to keep the addiction alive prevents the addict from seeking affiliative support. In other words, addicts often have special problems getting support because the addiction itself makes support that much more difficult to access.

Addicts often have special problems getting support because the addiction itself makes support that much more difficult to access.

Support and Treatment

Is there a difference between help and support, between help and treatment? In common parlance, support is often used to describe a shoulder to lean on, an emotional crutch, a sympathetic and understanding ear, or a friendly hand. When so defined, support is a general category that encompasses specific forms of help.

It could be argued that *any* form of help that is specifically aimed at changing a behavior is treatment, but treatment is more usually thought of as a planned set of interventions provided by someone trained in that form of treatment. If placed on a continuum, treatment is the most planned, developed, and professionally delivered form of help. It is likely to be a drafted form of support. At the other end of the continuum lie the types of nonprofessional help and support available through a system of natural support. Self-help groups and organizations fall in the middle of the continuum. They are forms of help that bridge the gap between nonprofessional help and professional treatment.

You can see that there is a great deal of help out there. Although the needs of each individual are likely to vary, most addicts will need multiple forms of support that run right along the continuum. When it comes to getting help for addiction, then, the question is not what help is available but rather:

Seeking, receiving, and accepting support are very much determined by who you are, what you expect, and how you see yourself in the world.

- What kind of help do you *need*?
- What kind of help do you *want*?
- Do you know *where* to get help?
- Do you know *how* to get help?
- Will you *accept* help when available?

Getting Support

As you move through your recovery, you'll need to determine how much and what type of support and where you can find it. Seeking, receiving, and accepting support are very much determined by who you are, what you expect, and how you see yourself in the world. But no matter how much trouble you may have asking for or accepting support, it's difficult to imagine that you've *never* received help or support. Use the next journal entry to think about getting support, and what it has meant in the past.

A FRIENDLY HAND

1. Think back to an instance from any period in your life when you needed support and got the support you needed. Describe that time in your life.

_____

_____

_____

_____

_____

_____

2. Why did you need support?

_____

_____

_____

3. Who provided that support?

_____

_____

_____

4. What type of support was provided?

_____

_____

_____

5. How did it help? If it didn't help, describe why not.

_____

_____

_____

6. What was it like to get support?

_____

_____

_____

_____

_____

7. Looking back at the support you received, what are you most grateful for?

_____

_____

_____

_____

_____

8. What might things have been like for you had you not received support?

_____

_____

_____

_____

_____

THINGS TO THINK ABOUT

- Was it easy to recall a time when you got support, or did you really have to stretch your memory? Are you someone who easily asks for support or accepts it?
- Do you let people know when you need support? What kind of support do you need right now?
- What would life be like without support from others? (If you're someone who doesn't get much support, what *is* life like without support?) Is this how you want life to be?

Obstacles to Support

There are many reasons people don't get the support they need and deserve.

- Sometimes we expect others to know we need support, even though we won't tell them or ask for support.

- It can be frightening to ask for help, because perhaps we're afraid we won't get it even though we've asked.

- The way we're raised and cultural expectations can get in the way of asking for or accepting help. For men especially, asking for or accepting help may not fit the self-image they've been taught to hold.

- Pride can get in the way of letting people know you need help. It may feel like admitting to a weakness.

- Like pride, shame can also get in the way. It can feel humiliating to ask for help. It can also feel like you're admitting to some personal failing.

- Sometimes people don't know help is available or don't know how to get it.

- Denial can get in the way because denial prevents you from asking. After all, asking for help means having to admit to a problem.

Use the next entry to think about how you approach, seek out, or accept support.

BARRIERS TO SUPPORT

1. How can you tell when you need support or help?

_____

_____

_____

_____

_____

2. When you need support, do you seek it out?

_____

_____

_____

_____

_____

3. When offered support, do you accept it?

_____

_____

_____

_____

_____

4. Name five things that interfere with your willingness to let people know you need support or help or your ability to accept it when offered:

a. _____

b. _____

c. _____

d. _____

e. _____

5. Whose help have you accepted? Why?

_____

_____

_____

_____

_____

_____

6. Whose help haven't you accepted? Why not?

_____

_____

_____

_____

_____

_____

7. Write a few words on the place of support and help in your life right now.

_____

_____

_____

_____

_____

_____

THINGS TO THINK ABOUT

- Can you ask for help when you need it? Do you *know* when you need help?
- Are you getting the kind of help you need at this time in your life? Are you accepting the kind of help you need?
- What's the *greatest* barrier to getting support right now?

Matching Support to Needs

To get effective help (that is, help that helps), you have to match your needs with the right kind of help. Sometimes when people are seeking help and support, they set themselves (and their helpers) up for failure. They have expectations that cannot be met, they seek attention from the wrong people or in the wrong places, or they ask for what they cannot have. Consequently, they are disappointed and unsatisfied. Their lives become a self-fulfilling prophecy: they expect to be disappointed and are because they're looking for the right things in the wrong places. This problem is compounded for addicts who have a demonstrated pattern of turning to the wrong kind of help (their addiction) to solve problems or satisfy needs. The failure to get *appropriate* help can lead to further feelings of inadequacy, aloneness, and frustration, which may send the addict off on a side road leading straight back to old patterns of addiction. This is addiction's vicious cycle.

The next journal entry will help you consider what kind of help is out there for you and how to get it, but remember, you must first decide you *want* help.

To get effective help (that is, help that helps), you have to match your needs with the right kind of help.

REACHING OUT

1. *I need help with . . .*

__family issues   __my marriage   __my relationships

__financial issues   __my mental health   __the way I feel

__legal issues   __my moods   __ the way I organize my life

__my addiction   __my physical health   __the way I think

other: _____   _____

_____   _____

_____   _____

2. What do you want in a helper?

___advice and guidance

___concrete direction setting

___experience helping people like me

___help available to me whenever I
    need it

___nonjudgmental attitude

___professional training

___warmth and understanding

___someone with a similar background
    to mine

other: _____

_____

_____

_____

_____

_____

_____

3. Who's available to give you support?

___addiction counselor

___attorney

___clergy/minister

___community mental health center

___coworkers

___counseling group

___counselor/therapist

___employee assistance program

___family members

___family physician/health care provider

___financial adviser

___friends

___hospital/addictin treatment center

___phone hotlines

___recovered addicts

___self-help groups

___school guidance or counseling services

___spiritual adviser

___supervisors (work)

___teachers (school)

other: _____

_____

_____

_____

_____

_____

_____

_____

4. Who are you ready to turn to for support right now? Make a list of the actual people you're willing to turn to for help. Next to each name, write what type of support or help you'll be asking for or hoping to get from that person.

Name   Type of Help Needed or Wanted

_____   _____

_____   _____

_____   _____

_____   _____

_____   _____

_____   _____

_____   _____

_____   _____

_____   _____

_____   _____

5. Can you let each person on your list know you need help? What about them (and you) makes communicating with them possible? If you can't, what prevents you?

_____

_____

_____

_____

6. What is most likely to prevent you from getting the kind of help you've identified needing?

_____

_____

_____

_____

7. What will happen if you don't get the help you need?

_____

_____

_____

_____

_____

THINGS TO THINK ABOUT

- It's relatively easy to write down your ideas and best intentions but often much harder to live out these ideas. Will you actually seek out help, or will you find reasons not to?
- Do you really want help? Are you really ready to give up your addiction and get the help you need to give it up?

Putting Thoughts into Action

Look through your local phone book for addiction counselors, therapists, and self-help groups. Then make contact.

Some sources of drafted help may come from the Internet, professional counselors, and self-help groups. Take the next two weeks to look through your local phone book for addiction counselors, therapists, and self-help groups. *Then make contact.*

Call two or three counselors or therapists and ask them about their philosophy and approach to treating addictions. In many cities and towns, there are local mental health agencies or clinics with addiction specialists. Also contact the self-help groups that focus on your addiction, ask about meetings, and plan to attend at least one meeting. Calling counselors and attending self-help meetings allow you to remain anonymous while simply checking things out. If you have access to the Internet, take some additional time to explore the sources of help, knowledge, or inspiration that might be available there.

If you think your addiction is too big for you to overcome alone, contact your family physician and see what help he or she can offer or suggest. If you're involved in the religious or spiritual community, contact your minister. If you're not ready to come out of the addiction closet with your doctor or minister, then call some addiction treatment centers that have inpatient or residential (live-in) programs.

To successfully complete this chapter, you must come away from it with a clear sense of the range of help that is available to you, from the informal and nonprofessional type to the formal and professional kind. Use the next journal entry to think about what types of *formal* self-help or professional help you will consider.

GETTING HELP

1. What kinds of help/support do you need in your life now? Check off all areas that apply, and add others below.

___affiliative help (companionship, connection with others, sense of belonging)

___counseling help (professional guidance, assistance, and direction)

___financial help (help with economic issues and concerns)

___legal help (addressing or resolving legal problems caused by or related to addiction)

___medical help (physical or health problems related to your addiction)

___mental health help (moods, thinking, and feelings)

___mentoring help (guidance/direction from others who have experienced similar problems)

___personal support (encouragement, understanding, a friendly shoulder, being cared for) __relationship help (help with family and friendships)

__spiritual help (spiritual or religious needs, connections to a larger community or plane)

__vocational help (school or work difficulties; problems finding work or entering school)

other: _____

_____

_____

_____

2. Revisit the list of possible support you identified in the Reaching Out journal entry you completed earlier in this chapter. Have you found even more sources of support from that list? What are they?

_____   _____

_____   _____

_____   _____

_____   _____

3. Match your needs with the support available. For each of your current help needs, identify the most likely sources for and types of help.

Type of Help Needed
(from Question 1 above)

Most Likely Sources of Help
(from Question 3 on page 104 and Question 2 above)

affiliative help   _____

counseling help   _____

financial help   _____

legal help   _____

medical help   _____

mental health help   _____

mentoring help   _____

personal support   _____

relationship help   _____

spiritual help   _____

vocational help   _____

other: _____   _____

_____   _____

_____   _____

_____   _____

4. Are you willing to do more research on self-help groups and organizations, professional counseling, or other *formal* types of help? Check off any forms of help you're willing to pursue right now, and add others below.

__attending a self-help group meeting   __meeting a therapist

__checking into an addiction treatment center   __talking to a minister or spiritual adviser

__meeting an addiction counselor   __meeting a school counselor

__meeting an employee assistance counselor   __talking to a physician/health care provider

other: _____   _____

_____   _____

_____   _____

_____   _____

5. If you're not willing to seek out formal types of help, what is stopping you?

_____

_____

_____

_____

_____

- Do you need help with your addiction? Are you ready to get help? Are you ready to get the *right* kind of help?
- Are you able to name the kind of help you need but still unable to actually *pursue* the right kind of help? If so, what's stopping you? What will it take for you to be able to overcome these barriers to getting help?

Final Thoughts

Your journal is a great tool to supplement formal help because it allows you to write and reflect on self-help meetings, counseling or therapy sessions, and so on. Use the next journal entry to record your thoughts about any meetings or sessions you attend. Use this entry every time you attend a group or session. Your journal can help you make better sense of the meeting, and you may find that you choose to share your thoughts in future meetings.

WRITING ABOUT HELP

Date of meeting or session: _____

1. Describe the meeting or session.

_____

_____

_____

_____

_____

_____

2. Was the experience useful? If it was, describe how. If it wasn't, why not?

_____

_____

_____

_____

_____

3. What was the most important or powerful thing you learned?

_____

_____

_____

_____

_____

4. Are there issues, ideas, or feelings you need to think more about before your next meeting or session?

_____

_____

_____

_____

_____

5. Are there issues, ideas, thoughts, or feelings you want to raise at your next meeting or session?

_____

_____

_____

_____

_____

6. Can this person or group offer continued help?

_____

_____

_____

_____

7. Will you continue to attend this group or see this person? If so, why? If not, why not?

_____

_____

_____

_____

_____

THINGS TO THINK ABOUT

- Is it useful to write about a group, meeting, or session after it's over?
- How will you decide whether to stay with this type of help or leave it? If you don't find it important or satisfying, are there alternative groups or people you can see for help?

Committing to Change

You've been thinking a lot about your addiction and have even begun reaching out to potential sources of help. But are you committed *to change?*

Now you must decide if you are ready to leave the early stages of recovery and move into the first stage that can be considered true recovery. You've been thinking a lot about your addiction and have even begun reaching out to potential sources of help. But are you *committed* to change?

It may seem strange to be this far into this book and only now be asked to make a commitment to overcoming your addiction. But all too often addicts go through the motions of recovery without genuinely working through the necessary steps. If you can honestly say you've done all the work, you're now ready for commitment.

Use the next journal entry to assess whether you're really ready and willing to maintain sobriety. Although sobriety is often associated with alcohol or drug use, it has a more general meaning that refers to acts of temperance, moderation, restraint, and self-control. These are exactly the characteristics and behaviors required in recovery. If you're *not* ready to commit yourself to sobriety, then you're not ready for recovery. If this is the case, return to Chapter 2 and work your way back through the last few chapters. Continue thinking about when you *will* be ready to stop or change your addictive behaviors.

CONSIDERING SOBRIETY

1. What's important in your life right now?

_____

_____

_____

_____

_____

_____

2. Describe the effects of your addiction on your life.

_____

_____

_____

_____

_____

3. Describe the effects of your addiction on the lives of others.

_____

_____

_____

_____

_____

4. What might happen if you modified or stopped the behaviors that are causing problems? How might your life change?

_____

_____

_____

_____

_____

5. Do you want to end your addiction?

_____

_____

_____

6. Are you ready to commit to ending your addiction?

_____

_____

_____

7. Check off your goals for sobriety, and add others below.

___abstinence (total avoidance of addictive behaviors), *temporary*

___abstinence (total avoidance of addictive behaviors), *permanent*

___moderation (reduction of and greater control over addictive behaviors)

other: _____

_____

8. What dead ends or side roads are out there for you? What will lead you back to active addiction?

_____

_____

_____

9. What must you do to avoid these dead ends and side roads?

_____

_____

_____

THINGS TO THINK ABOUT

- Are you ready for sobriety? If not, what will it take to become ready?
- If you've chosen temporary abstinence or moderation, instead of permanent abstinence, are you being realistic or avoiding _really_ dealing with the problems of your addiction? Are you hoping that you can overcome your addiction and later return to the same old behaviors?

Contracting for Sobriety

The final entry in this chapter represents a contract with yourself to enter sobriety and _remain_ sober. As is the case with any contract, once signed the intention is to stick with its terms.

The most useful way to use this contract is to review and recommit to it daily. Accordingly, make a copy of the contract and place it somewhere you can see it every day. Tape it to a mirror in your bathroom, put it in your wallet or purse, give a copy to your spouse or partner, or post it on the steering wheel of your car. In other words, put it somewhere where you will see it each and every day as you enter Stage 3 of your recovery and move toward early (and then active) recovery.

A CONTRACT FOR SOBRIETY

The date I enter sobriety: _____

Think carefully about each of the following statements before you check off your agreement.

___ I will meet my goals of abstinence or moderation.

___ I will accept the discomfort and pain of recovery.

___ I will stay connected with important people in my life.

___ I will seek and accept support.

___ I will be honest with myself and others.

___ I will read this contract each and every day.

___ I won't expect recovery to be easy.

___ I won't try to escape from my discomfort and pain through my addiction.

___ I won't hide my behavior from important people in my life.

___ I won't try to predict how long it will take to feel better.

___ I won't lie to myself or others.

___ I won't ignore this contract with myself and pretend it doesn't exist.

_____   _____

Signature   Date

"The secret of success is
constancy to purpose."
—BENJAMIN
DISRAELI

7

Destination:

ADDICTION-FREE—

THE DAY YOU STOP

JULES

*I can't really pin down the day I became addicted. I can remember
when I first started using, and actually the people I started using
with, but not the time and the moment that I actually became addicted. I'm sure that's impossible. But I sure can remember the day I
stopped.*

*Actually I stopped many times, but only once did I actually stop
and mean it. I'll always remember that day.*

THIS CHAPTER CONTAINS a simple idea—the essence of your entire journey through addiction to recovery. At the end of the previous chapter, you signed a contract for sobriety. Now you have
to live it out, each and every day.

What Sort of Sobriety?

The first journal entry in this chapter will help you to think about
whether your decision to stop, and how you *plan* to stop, is realistic. Remember, "stopping" will be different for different people.

For some, it means complete and lifelong abstinence, but for others it may mean significantly modifying their addictive behaviors. For many addicts, moderation is not a realistic choice, so focus on candor and honesty as you work on this entry.

YOUR DECISION

1. Are you choosing abstinence (completely stopping) or simply modifying your behaviors as your means to recovery? Why do you think this choice is appropriate for you?

_____

_____

_____

2. Are you making permanent or temporary changes?

_____

_____

_____

3. What are your long-term goals?

_____

_____

_____

4. Name three important people in your life:

a. _____

b. _____

c. _____

5. Ask each person if he or she agrees with:

- your decision to enter abstinence or modify your behaviors
- your decision to make permanent or temporary changes
- your long-term goals

Record their responses here.

_____

_____

_____

_____

_____

6. If you're modifying your behaviors instead of becoming _completely_ abstinent, are you being realistic? Are you kidding yourself? Explain.

_____

_____

_____

7. Are you ready for sobriety? Explain.

_____

_____

_____

_____

THINGS TO THINK ABOUT

- Do you listen to or disregard the feelings and advice of friends and family?
- Can you count on friends and family to help you as you enter recovery? Will you _use_ their help?

The Day You Stop

Use this journal entry to record the day you stopped. It will be one of the most important days in your life.

ON THIS DAY

On _____, I became sober.

              day and date

1. *On this day I feel . . .* _____

_____

_____

_____

_____

2. *On this day, I look forward to . . .* _____

_____

_____

_____

_____

3. *On this day, I remember . . .* _____

_____

_____

_____

4. *On this day, I say to myself . . .* _____

_____

_____

_____

5. *For each and every day that follows, I will remember . . .* _____

_____

_____

_____

_____

6. For each and every day that follows, I will tell myself... _____

_____

_____

_____

7. Describe this day.

_____

_____

_____

_____

_____

_____

_____

THINGS TO THINK ABOUT

- Does stopping feel real? Are you worried it's only temporary?
- What can you do to increase the chances that stopping is permanent? Who can you turn to?
- Are you aware of the consequences of returning to addiction? Do you have a relapse prevention plan?

The First Thirty Days

Recovery is a lifelong process, but the first thirty days are among the most fragile. At thirty days your recovery is far from complete, but your first month will mark a milestone in your recovery. Use this chapter's final journal entry each and every day for the next thirty days to remind yourself of this day and of your contract for sobriety.

Recovery is a lifelong process, but the first thirty days are among the most fragile.

THIRTY DAYS

"A minute's success pays the failure of years."
—ROBERT BROWNING

	Date	Your Initials
Day 1: I have read and renewed my contract for sobriety:	_____	_____
Day 2: I have read and renewed my contract for sobriety:	_____	_____
Day 3: I have read and renewed my contract for sobriety:	_____	_____
Day 4: I have read and renewed my contract for sobriety:	_____	_____
Day 5: I have read and renewed my contract for sobriety:	_____	_____
Day 6: I have read and renewed my contract for sobriety:	_____	_____
Day 7: I have read and renewed my contract for sobriety:	_____	_____
Day 8: I have read and renewed my contract for sobriety:	_____	_____
Day 9: I have read and renewed my contract for sobriety:	_____	_____
Day 10: I have read and renewed my contract for sobriety:	_____	_____
Day 11: I have read and renewed my contract for sobriety:	_____	_____
Day 12: I have read and renewed my contract for sobriety:	_____	_____
Day 13: I have read and renewed my contract for sobriety:	_____	_____
Day 14: I have read and renewed my contract for sobriety:	_____	_____
Day 15: I have read and renewed my contract for sobriety:	_____	_____
Day 16: I have read and renewed my contract for sobriety:	_____	_____
Day 17: I have read and renewed my contract for sobriety:	_____	_____
Day 18: I have read and renewed my contract for sobriety:	_____	_____
Day 19: I have read and renewed my contract for sobriety:	_____	_____
Day 20: I have read and renewed my contract for sobriety:	_____	_____
Day 21: I have read and renewed my contract for sobriety:	_____	_____

Day 22: I have read and renewed my contract for sobriety: _____   _____

Day 23: I have read and renewed my contract for sobriety: _____   _____

Day 24: I have read and renewed my contract for sobriety: _____   _____

Day 25: I have read and renewed my contract for sobriety: _____   _____

Day 26: I have read and renewed my contract for sobriety: _____   _____

Day 27: I have read and renewed my contract for sobriety: _____   _____

Day 28: I have read and renewed my contract for sobriety: _____   _____

Day 29: I have read and renewed my contract for sobriety: _____   _____

Day 30: I have read and renewed my contract for sobriety: _____   _____

Day 31: I will continue living by my contract for sobriety: _____   _____

THINGS TO THINK ABOUT

- Would it help to *keep* renewing your contract daily for another thirty days?
- Is it getting easier to live by your contract with each passing day or more difficult? Either way, why?

Destination:

RELAPSE AND SLIPS

BARRY

*I was definitely one of those people who thought I could stop any-
time I wanted, but I just wasn't quite ready. Each time I stopped, I
started again. And each time, I had a great reason. Actually, because I was so hard on myself, I had to come up with excuses for not
being able to quit. It wasn't until I came to grips with things and
realized that I had to stop but couldn't that I came to see all those
failed attempts as relapses. I hated the word at first, because for me
it spelled failure—not being good or strong enough.*

*The funny thing is, being strong really meant admitting I wasn't
as strong as I wanted to be. Only after I could admit to relapse,
which meant admitting to addiction, was I able to stop being so
hard on myself and instead get tough on addiction. Then, and only
then, could I develop and use a relapse prevention plan and begin
to move on with my recovery, relapses and all.*

IT'S TOO EASY to think that recovery is just a matter of willpower
alone. If it were that easy, few people would remain addicted

once they chose to quit. As Mark Twain once noted, "I know I can quit smoking because I've done it a thousand times."

Changing habits is difficult under the best of circumstances; for addicts change is even more difficult. It's important to realize from the outset that slips and relapses are inevitable for most people. However, these slips don't signal the end of recovery but are simply setbacks along the way. Learning how to recover from a slip provides an opportunity for even stronger recovery. In the words of playwright Tom Stoppard, "Every exit is an entry somewhere else."

Relapses and Slips

A relapse and a slip are similar. Both represent a return to addictive behavior, although in differing degrees of regression. A slip is more like a stumble whereas a relapse is closer to a plunge. Neither is necessarily part of your journey. Some people in recovery manage to avoid relapses and slips completely, but many others will experience at least one kind or another. Although slips and relapses can pose a significant risk, they are to be avoided, not feared. If treated as learning experiences rather than failures, they become "detours" along the road—and an important part of your growth.

One way to guard against these setbacks is to be aware of the events that trigger them. Also, you should have a prevention plan in place before a relapse or slip occurs.

Triggers

Certain memories, relationships, behaviors, and situations are connected to specific thoughts and feelings. For instance, hearing a song may evoke happy memories; seeing an old flame may cause feelings of jealousy to erupt. Positive feelings tend to result in positive behaviors, negative feelings in negative ones.

Although slips and relapses can pose a significant risk, they are to be avoided, not feared. If treated as learning experiences rather than failures, they become "detours" along the road—and an important part of your growth.

The important thing is this: you can do something about your thoughts and feelings. If being around family makes you feel safe and comfortable, then you know that this is a good place to be if you're feeling anxious. If passing a certain landmark on your way to work brings back sad and depressing memories, you can change your route to work. Knowing your "triggers" allows you to take more control over your life.

Triggers are those things in your life that activate or arouse thoughts, feelings, and reactions. They can be people, sounds, smells, situations, or behaviors—anything that brings back memories or feelings. Triggers that stimulate good feelings are to be embraced; triggers that stimulate negative feelings are to be avoided. Your feelings and thoughts are predictable, but you must learn to recognize what triggers them.

Your feelings and thoughts are predictable, but you must learn to recognize what triggers them.

Relapse Triggers

Passing a favorite bar on the way home from the movies may prompt an alcoholic to go in and have a drink. For the smoker, having a stressful meeting at work may evoke the desire for a cigarette. Watching others eat chocolate cake is likely to elicit cravings for the food addict. In these examples, each situation represents a trigger and invitation to slipping or relapsing.

Behaviors can also serve as triggers. For the sex addict, engaging in flirting behavior may be the "gateway" behavior that leads to an inappropriate or unhealthy sexual encounter. Many believe that the use of "soft" drugs such as alcohol or marijuana serves as a gateway to harder drugs such as heroin or cocaine. Attending a party and offering to hold someone's drink is a surefire gateway behavior to having a drink yourself.

Some events may be *associatively* linked to previous addictive behaviors. For example, festive holidays are accompanied by a great deal of drinking or eating, and in the addict's mind they

Some events may be associatively linked to previous addictive behaviors. . . . Perhaps you associate parties with sex, summer vacations with major spending sprees, a sporting event with heavy gambling, or a rock concert with drugs.

provide a "reasonable" opportunity to get drunk or overeat. Perhaps you associate parties with sex, summer vacations with major spending sprees, a sporting event with heavy gambling, or a rock concert with drugs.

For some people, relationships trigger the addictive urge. Perhaps a friend *actively* encourages you to engage in the behavior. Maybe a difficult relationship triggers addictive behaviors: your spouse infuriates you and "drives" you to get high or your supervisor gives you a difficult assignment at work. Memories too can serve as triggers: the anniversary of a death, the memory of the fun you always had when you got drunk, the rush you felt when betting on the horses.

Some situations, events, and relationships will always be high risk for you because of the connection to your addiction. You don't have to avoid them (though you may choose to), but you must learn to be *aware* of these connections and their possible (or likely) impact on your addiction. This awareness can help you make reasonable and careful decisions that will support recovery and help you avoid slips and relapses.

The next entry will help you think about those things that trigger thoughts, feelings, and cravings.

TRIGGERS

1. Are there certain types of situations that trigger cravings to engage in your addiction?

_____

_____

_____

_____

_____

_____

2. Are there certain people who trigger cravings?

_____

_____

_____

_____

_____

3. Are there things besides situations and people that are triggers for you—sights, smells, sounds?

_____

_____

_____

_____

_____

4. What emotions or thoughts do these things trigger?

_____

_____

_____

_____

_____

5. Why do these things trigger these feelings and thoughts?

_____

_____

_____

_____

_____

_____

High-Risk Situations

Certain situations can increase the likelihood that addicts will experience cravings to use or engage in their addiction. Are these situations familiar to you?

Certain situations can increase the likelihood that addicts will experience cravings to use or engage in their addiction.

- Others are engaging in behaviors that are addictive for you.
- There is direct pressure on you to engage in addictive behaviors.
- You are enjoying yourself, but using or engaging in addictive behaviors would enhance your pleasure.
- You are *not* enjoying yourself, but using or engaging in addictive behaviors would improve your mood and boost your confidence.
- You feel left out or unable to join in without the high or feeling of satisfaction provided by your addiction.
- You feel fatigued, physically or emotionally, and using or engaging in addictive behaviors would stimulate you.
- Negative feelings are taking over and engaging in addictive behaviors would help you to cope.
- You are bored and feel that engaging in addictive behaviors would stimulate you.

These situations, as well as the people, places, and times that are connected to them combine to create an environment that promotes relapse. It is not the situations themselves that are high risk but instead the associations they have with your addiction and the way you respond to them. Building on the previous journal entry, use the next entry to create a list of people, places, times, and situations that pose a risk to your recovery.

DANGEROUS LIAISONS

1. What people or relationships in your life are high risk for you? Why?

Who	Why
_____	_____
_____	_____
_____	_____
_____	_____
_____	_____
_____	_____

2. What times of the day, the week, the month, or the year are high risk for you? Why?

When	Why
_____	_____
_____	_____
_____	_____
_____	_____
_____	_____
_____	_____

3. What places, locations, parts of town, or parts of your home are high risk for you? Why?

Where	Why

4. What situations are high risk for you? Why?

What	Why

5. What else represents a high-risk situation for you? Why?

Trigger	Why

6. What can you do to avoid these high-risk people, places, times, or situations or to minimize their risk to you?

_____

_____

_____

_____

_____

_____

_____

_____

7. What can you do to minimize the relapse triggering effects of these dangerous liaisons when you *can't* avoid them?

_____

_____

_____

_____

_____

_____

_____

_____

THINGS TO THINK ABOUT

- Must you avoid these triggers forever or just until you fully enter recovery?
- Will you miss the people, places, and things you may have to give up in recovery, or will you be well rid of them?
- What replacement behaviors must you develop to take the place of the addiction you've come to depend on in social situations?

Cravings

Because relapses are often preceded by cravings, cravings serve to warn of a possible relapse.

Because relapses are often preceded by cravings, cravings serve to warn of a possible relapse. If you use the next journal entry when you're experiencing a craving, it may help you avoid giving in to the feeling. Repeat this entry each time a craving strikes.

AVOIDING THE FALL

1. What are you craving?

_____

2. Describe your craving in words.

_____

_____

_____

_____

3. What triggered this craving?

_____

_____

_____

4. Reread the Contract for Sobriety you signed in Chapter 6. Remind yourself why you signed that contract and write about those reasons.

_____

_____

_____

_____

_____

5. What can you do to satisfy this craving other than engaging in the addiction?

_____

_____

_____

_____

_____

6. What can you do to distract yourself and avoid the craving?

_____

_____

_____

_____

_____

7. What can you do to ride out, weather, or tolerate the craving?

_____

_____

_____

_____

_____

8. Remind yourself of the reasons to enter and stay in recovery. What will happen if you give in to this craving? What will the immediate consequences be?

_____

_____

_____

_____

_____

_____

9. What might the larger consequences be if you relapse?

_____

_____

_____

_____

_____

_____

_____

_____

THINGS TO THINK ABOUT

- Did it help to write about the consequences of relapse *before* you slipped? What was the most useful part of writing about your cravings?
- Did you relapse anyway? If so, how are you feeling at the moment? If not, how are you feeling?
- How will you deal with recurring episodes of craving?

Rationalizations

When people do slip, they often rationalize their behavior in some way. "I've done so well for so long, I deserve a little reward." "What harm will a *little* slip do anyway? I can always go back to sobriety later." "I had a hard day." And so on.

Use the next journal entry to come to grips with all those reasons and excuses for relapsing. It may seem odd to give reasons for *staying* addicted and giving in to cravings, but you may as well confront your rationalizations now. Once they are put to paper you'll be able to challenge them and appreciate the reasons *not* to relapse.

EXCUSES, EXCUSES

1. List five reasons for keeping your addiction.

a. _____

b. _____

c. _____

d. _____

e. _____

2. List five reasons for not getting help before you relapse.

a. _____

b. _____

c. _____

d. _____

e. _____

3. List five excuses for giving in to your craving and relapsing back into addiction.

a. _____

b. _____

c. _____

d. _____

e. _____

4. What do you make of all these rationalizations and excuses?

_____

_____

_____

_____

_____

_____

5. List ten reasons to stay in recovery.

a. _____

b. _____

c. _____

d. _____

e. _____

f. _____

g. _____

h. _____

i. _____

j. _____

6. Are you still committed to recovery? Explain.

_____

_____

_____

_____

_____

_____

_____

_____

_____

_____

THINGS TO THINK ABOUT

- Are there more reasons to stay in recovery or more reasons to relapse?
- What gets in the way of remembering the reasons to stay in recovery when you're experiencing a craving? How can you remind yourself of the reasons to stay in recovery?

Expressing Yourself

A major theme of this book is self-expression. Feelings can be so explosive at times that you must let them out. Whether your feelings are negative or positive, letting them out is usually healthy. It's *how* you let them out that can be problematic.

People can let their feelings out by talking to someone, engaging in a physical activity, or expressing themselves through art or writing. Self-expression generally refers to the deliberate, controlled release of feelings. When you express yourself, you not only vent your feelings, but you also give shape to them. Consider the words of the Italian playwright Ugo Betti: "Thought itself needs words. It runs on them like a long wire. And if it loses the habit of words, little by little it becomes shapeless, somber."

Whether you've given in to a craving or managed to avoid the slip, use the next journal entry to describe your feelings.

Whether your feelings are negative or positive, letting them out is usually healthy. It's how *you let them out that can be problematic.*

AFTERWARD

"Words are, of course, the most powerful drug used by mankind."
—RUDYARD KIPLING

1. If you gave in to your craving, write about your feelings *at this moment*. If you've been able to deny the craving, write about your feelings *at this moment*.

_____

_____

_____

_____

_____

_____

_____

_____

_____

_____

_____

_____

2. *I feel . . .* _____

_____

3. *Next time I feel a craving . . .* _____

_____

4. *Now I need to . . .* _____

_____

Warning Signs

Addicts are remarkably adept at masking, or covering up, their feelings. After entering recovery, however, they often begin to reexperience once-buried feelings.

Cravings are those *urges* to once again engage in addictive behaviors: those fond reminiscences of how good it felt, that need to avoid or escape the present, or those physical or emotional feelings that you just *have* to use again or reengage in the activity that seemed to make everything better (but of course didn't).

Besides cravings, people experience a number of warning signs before relapsing. These warnings may take the form of rationalizing thoughts or negative, overwhelming emotions. Addicts are remarkably adept at masking, or covering up, their feelings. After entering recovery, however, they often begin to reexperience once-buried feelings. Think about whether any of these warning signs apply to you.

- *Denial.* You return to the idea that you really don't have a problem.

- *Despair.* Nothing is any good and things don't seem to be improving.

- *Disbelief.* You decide that you really don't have such a serious problem or can take care of it without having to enter recovery.

- *Disillusionment.* Even though you're in recovery, life doesn't seem any better.

- *Disregard.* You stop caring about the consequences, or what anyone else thinks.

- *Doubt.* You're not sure that recovery is really the way to improve your life.

- *Failure.* You've relapsed already, perhaps more than once, and you'll probably slip again anyway.

- *Giving up.* You feel this is just too difficult.

- *Helplessness.* You feel you can't do this or can't handle life without your addiction to help you along.

- *Impatience.* Your recovery isn't moving as quickly as you want it to.

- *Intolerance.* You can't put up with the feelings, the work, or the deprivation and sacrifice required in recovery.

- *Lack of confidence.* You doubt you have the skills or the character required to be successful in either recovery or life in general.

- *Loss of interest.* You no longer feel it's important to enter or stay in recovery.

- *Low self-esteem.* You feel pretty badly about yourself.

- *Overconfidence.* You're feeling confident and capable that you can *easily* manage recovery.

- *Overwhelmed.* Feelings, thoughts, doubts, and pressures seem to just be washing all over you.

- *Resentment.* You feel irritated and imposed upon by having to give up something so important to you. You feel it's not fair when you see others engaging in their addictions.

- *Self-doubt.* You don't think you have what it takes, you're nothing without your addiction, you can't do it alone.

- *Self-pity.* Your life is tough, and depriving yourself of the one thing that helps is just too hard and plain unfair.

- *Shame.* You find it hard to face the damage to self or others that may have been caused by your addiction.

These sentiments do not always indicate a possible relapse. Many addicts, new to recovery, will experience them too. That the very thoughts and feelings that accompany recovery can also signal relapse illustrates how easy it is to flee from recovery back into addiction.

Relapse Prevention Techniques

It's not enough to simply *know* you may be facing a slip. Equally important is having alternatives in place that can serve as a substitute for your addiction, as a diversion, or as a way to delay relapse so that you can control your feelings or get outside help.

- Delay the urge by finding ways to put off the act of using or engaging.

- Reduce the urge by imagining that you're "kicking" the urge away, letting the urge pass through you like a wind, or riding it like a surfer riding a wave.

- Imagine doing something else you enjoy and find satisfying. Imagine a pleasant scene and being in that scene.

- Find alternative behaviors and engage in alternative activities that can substitute for the addiction, prove satisfying, and dissipate the demands and urges associated with the craving: take a walk, talk to someone, write in your journal, write a letter, listen to music, have a cup of tea, play football, go swimming, run a mile, go out dancing, or go to a movie.

- Get help. Turn to a family member, friend, or supporter, or contact a counselor or hotline.

- Say aloud mastery statements as a way of conquering and dissipating urges: "I can do this." "I'm more powerful than this urge." "Urges never hurt anyone." "This urge will pass, but I'll still be here."

Find alternative behaviors and engage in alternative activities that can substitute for the addiction, prove satisfying, and dissipate the demands and urges associated with the craving.

Planning for Relapse Prevention

Think about the signs that may signal a pending relapse for you and the techniques and activities that you can use to stave off a possible relapse. Put a plan in place *now* that you can fall back on should a relapse seem possible. Your plan should address the following:

- Identify those thoughts, ideas, feelings, or experiences that may trigger urges or forewarn you of possible relapse.

- Describe the techniques you can use to push away, reduce, or delay relapse.

- List activities and things you can do to substitute for the addiction and dissipate the power of urges.

- Map out people and resources you can turn to and fall back on to help get you through the urges without slipping back into addictive behaviors.

Use the next journal entry to draft your plan. Remember, your plan will be effective only if you use it.

A MAP FOR RELAPSE PREVENTION

1. Describe five signs that may be warnings of a pending slip or relapse.

a. _____

b. _____

c. _____

d. _____

e. _____

2. List five events, incidents, or difficulties in your daily life that might make you want to engage in your addiction.

a. _____

b. _____

c. _____

d. _____

e. _____

3. If you feel an urge to reengage in addiction, describe five things or thoughts you can focus on that can help distract or rechannel your urges elsewhere.

a. _____

b. _____

c. _____

d. _____

e. _____

4. List five activities you can do as alternatives to engaging in addictive behaviors.

a. _____

b. _____

c. _____

d. _____

e. _____

5. Who can you talk to or turn to for support if you feel like you may relapse?

a. _____

b. _____

c. _____

d. _____

e. _____

6. What other resources, such as counselors or hotlines, can you turn to if you become concerned about relapse?

a. _____

b. _____

c. _____

d. _____

e. _____

THINGS TO THINK ABOUT

- Is creating a relapse prevention plan an important task for you? Are you treating this plan seriously?
- Are you sufficiently satisfied with your recovery to think you don't need a relapse prevention plan? If so, does this fall under the category of "overconfidence"?
- Will you actually use your relapse prevention plan if it becomes necessary?

9

Destination:

UNDERSTANDING EMOTIONS

CAROLINE

I was driven by my emotions. Everything I did seemed an offshoot of how I was feeling. If I felt bad it was an excuse to do something to help feel better, and if I felt good it was an invitation to keep feeling good or feel even better. But many of my behaviors were more complicated than that, driven by an underground current of feelings, most of which were bad. I felt I could never do anything well, and almost everything that went wrong—or more to the point, everything that failed to make my life better—just fueled my compulsive eating and my drinking. I buried my feelings in food or alcohol and kept them buried. The worse I felt, the more I felt it was okay to eat or binge drink. The more I ate and drank, the worse I felt. After I started in group I realized the trick was to shut off that underground emotional current because it was washing me away.

RECOGNIZING AND DEALING with feelings is a crucial part of staying addiction free. In Chapter 7, you learned that many of the signs of imminent relapse are associated with feelings, and this is because addictions often serve to help people avoid painful feel-

147

ings. But addictions not only serve to cover up and bypass negative feelings, they also serve to artificially create, stimulate, or enhance good feelings.

Left without the addiction, the recovering addict is faced with a double problem—a swell of raw feelings that were formerly hidden and a lack of positive emotional experiences. Addicts are accustomed to immediate gratification because that is what their addiction gives them. A further challenge for the recovering addict is to find ways to remain patient and learn to defer instant *emotional* gratification. Those unable to tolerate and manage their own emotions are likely to slip back into addiction.

The Mask

Emotions are our unfiltered reactions and responses to the world around us and our relationships and interactions in that world.

Emotions are our unfiltered reactions and responses to the world around us and our relationships and interactions in that world. Although we can avoid situations that trigger negative emotions, our feelings nevertheless remain immune to our direct control. We can influence them through our choices and the situations into which we place ourselves, but we cannot command them. As inconvenient as this reality may be, emotions also serve a very useful purpose: they are the landscape within and outside us. If you're in touch with them, your emotions let you know what's going on inside as you interact with the world outside, and they can then provide the basis for effective decisions and choices. Willard Gaylin, the psychiatrist and ethicist, has described feelings as "the fine instruments which shape decision making."

Addictions have an unfortunate effect on feelings. They artificially manipulate emotions by repressing some and promoting others. They allow you to feel confident, they enhance sociability, and they enrich your experience of the world—all without any input from you (apart from your engaging in the addiction).

More often, however, they bypass or muzzle difficult and painful emotions, so you can forget your problems and avoid feelings of sadness or depression. Addictions mask emotions, and in their mind- or mood-altering way, they make you less powerful and limit your ability to be in charge of not only your emotions but your life. Addictions control you, and without access to your feelings, you lack a critical tool for *effective* decision making.

Emotional Gratification

Addictions provide immediate relief. Feel lousy? Smoke a cigarette, knock back a six-pack, eat a bar of chocolate, or buy ten lottery tickets. You don't have to work toward authentic emotional rewards because your addiction will provide artificial gratification instantly. If you've been addicted long enough, you may never have learned the skills that allow you to tolerate your emotions or defer immediate gratification. Just as infants want their needs met *now,* so too do many addicted adults. If you're going to stay in recovery, mastering the skills of tolerance, patience, and recognizing and managing emotions is crucial.

If you're going to stay in recovery, mastering the skills of tolerance, patience, and recognizing and managing emotions is crucial.

Managing Feelings

Managing feelings doesn't mean eliminating them, ignoring them, or allowing them to take over your life and control your every behavior and relationship, and it certainly doesn't mean filtering them through addictive behaviors to mask them. Personal development entails finding ways to deal with your emotions. First, however, you must learn to manage them.

+ *Tolerate the feeling* by accepting it, putting up with it, and finding a way to live with it no matter how unpleasant the feeling may be.

- *Cope with the pressure of the feeling* by finding a way to ensure that the feeling doesn't push you into behavior that you know is bad for you, bad for others, or in some other way inappropriate.

- *Listen to the feeling* by paying attention to and understanding the meaning of the emotion: why you're feeling this way, what's causing the feeling, and what the feeling is "telling" you about the situation.

- *Respond to the feeling* by finding an appropriate response to the feeling. Sometimes this means telling someone how you feel, other times taking a walk or being alone, sometimes crying and sometimes yelling, and sometimes not doing anything at all.

Ideally, you will put to use all four steps in sequence when dealing with your feelings in an emotionally changed climate. However, even if you don't make it to the second step, just tolerating the feeling can have great value.

Managing feelings ultimately involves responding appropriately to them. Inappropriate responses allow you to engage in self-defeating or self-destructive behaviors that are intended to eliminate the feeling. Responding appropriately will entail healthy self-expression.

Becoming Aware of Feelings

People usually don't have to manage pleasant feelings. It's the unpleasant ones that must be dealt with: sadness, bitterness, depression, anger, anxiety, shame, and guilt, to name a few. Everyone experiences these feelings at one time or another. Addicts are especially likely to do so after entering recovery.

Many people do a really good job of avoiding their feelings by pretending they're not there. Sometimes they recognize only a small subset of their feelings. They don't realize that their anger, for instance, is a reaction to feelings of rejection or abandonment, not just plain annoyance. Perhaps their feelings of depression are underpinned by feelings of failure, disappointment, and vulnerability. In other words, people sometimes confuse one feeling for another or are so used to experiencing only one or two feelings that they fail to see that feelings are often interconnected.

Use the next entry to help recognize and develop an inventory of the sort of feelings you experience and their causes. Think about *why* you experience a particular feeling.

People sometimes confuse one feeling for another or are so used to experiencing only one or two feelings that they fail to see that feelings are often interconnected.

MY FEELINGS

How I Feel   *Why I Feel This Way*

__afraid   _____

__amused   _____

__angry   _____

__anxious   _____

__ashamed   _____

__bitter   _____

__detached   _____

__disappointed _____

__foolish   _____

__guilty   _____

__happy   _____

__helpless   _____

__hopeful   _____

__hopeless   _____

__ignored   _____

__incapable

__irritated

__lonely

__numb

__overwhelmed

__sad

__trapped

__vulnerable

__worthless

__yearning

other: _____

_____

_____

_____

_____

_____

_____

_____

_____

_____

_____

_____

_____

_____

_____

_____

_____

_____

THINGS TO THINK ABOUT

- Were you easily able to pick out feelings? If you've used this journal entry more than once, is it getting easier to recognize your feelings?
- Do you understand why you feel the way you do? Does understanding your feelings help you regulate them?
- Do you think you need to complete journal entries like this one? If not, why have you had so much difficulty overcoming your addiction? Are you sure you're in touch with and can accurately recognize your emotions?

Recognizing and Understanding Feelings

Recognizing feelings is an important step in learning to manage them. *Interoceptive* awareness is the ability to correctly recognize and interpret feelings as you have them. People with poor interoceptive awareness often misidentify their feelings, but people whose interoceptive awareness is finely tuned understand *why* they feel the way they do. They're able to look inside and focus on their thoughts and feelings. Taking the time to think about your feelings and reflect on your thoughts is one way to better know yourself and adjust to the world around you. It also helps you stop your feelings from immediately being acted out as behaviors. Recognizing that you have a feeling becomes a buffer or a bridge between emotion and behavior.

Use the next entry to deal with one feeling at a time. It can be used for either difficult, painful feelings or positive, upbeat ones. Copy the blank entry for repeated use.

People with poor interoceptive awareness often misidentify their feelings, but people whose interoceptive awareness is finely tuned understand why they feel the way they do.

HOW DO YOU FEEL?

1. How are you feeling?

_____

_____

_____

_____

2. Describe the situation that led to the feeling.

_____

_____

_____

_____

3. Describe the feeling.

If this feeling had a color, it would be . . . _____

If this feeling had sound, it would be . . . _____

If this feeling had a scent, it would be . . . _____

If this feeling was an animal, it would be . . . _____

If this feeling had a texture, it would be . . . _____

I feel . . . _____

_____

_____

_____

4. Is this a common feeling for you?

_____

_____

_____

5. How do you usually respond to feelings like this?

_____

_____

_____

_____

6. Is there anything you *should* do about this feeling—anyone you should talk to or any action you should take?

_____

_____

_____

_____

7. Is there anything you *shouldn't* do about this feeling?

_____

_____

_____

_____

8. How can you best make use of this feeling?

_____

_____

_____

_____

THINGS TO THINK ABOUT

- Is this a difficult feeling to deal with? if so, does it ever get the better of you?
- Are there many feelings that are difficult for you to deal with or just one or two? In general, what helps most in dealing with difficult feelings?
- What can you learn from your feelings? What can you learn from *this* feeling?

Emotions, Behavior, and Thoughtfulness

Emotions have no independent power to act on the world outside of you. That is, until an emotion is transformed into an action, its actual impact is neither good nor bad. It's the *behaviors* provoked by an emotion that are judged as good, bad, or neutral by their actual consequences. Although we can't control our feelings, we *can*—and must—take responsibility for our behavior.

Behavior is what other people see—the outward expression of what's going on inside of you. It includes both what you do— yelling, crying, moping, getting angry, or laughing—as well as what you say. It also includes the things that people can observe about you, such as your attitude, body language, and how you spend your time. Finally, behavior also includes the things you *don't* do, like not saying hello to someone, not attending a meeting, or not finishing something you started. In other words, your behaviors include almost every facet of your interactions with the world and the people in it.

Emotions, good or bad, are not invitations to action. Just the

Although we can't control our feelings, we can—and must—take responsibility for our behavior.

opposite. They're a statement that something powerful is happening to you and a message to start thinking *before* acting.

Coping Behaviors

Knowing that you have feelings and being able to identify them is an important step in managing your emotions. Still, knowing you're angry or sad doesn't necessarily mean you know how to tolerate or deal with the feeling. It's your behavior that actually copes, or deals, with a feeling.

Coping behaviors are those things we do to help express and vent emotional pressure. Addiction is an example of a negative coping behavior, an *attempt* to cope that doesn't work. Effective coping behaviors *improve,* not worsen, your situation, and they strengthen your ability to deal with issues. Effective coping is always healthy and incorporates these elements:

Addiction is an example of a negative coping behavior, an attempt to cope that doesn't work.

- knowing when you have feelings—being in touch with what's going on inside
- identifying feelings—recognizing and being able to name the feelings
- tolerating feelings—accepting the feelings, and not trying to escape them
- managing feelings—controlling your feelings, not letting them control you
- understanding feelings— connecting your feelings to their causes
- expressing feelings—allowing your feelings to emerge and be expressed

Use the next entry to focus on your coping behaviors. Your writing will help you think about ways to deal with your feelings and behaviors to avoid when you experience difficult emotions.

COPING BEHAVIORS

1. How do you deal with your feelings?

_____

_____

_____

2. Can you tolerate difficult feelings?

_____

_____

_____

3. Do you give in to your feelings and act on them without thinking?

_____

_____

_____

4. Do you listen to your feelings and understand where they're coming from or what they're trying to tell you?

_____

_____

_____

5. Do you respond appropriately to your feelings?

_____

_____

_____

6. Which of your behavioral responses to your feelings are self-destructive or self-defeating?

_____

_____

_____

7. Which of your behaviors are the healthiest when it comes to dealing with your feelings?

_____

_____

_____

_____

_____

_____

THINGS TO THINK ABOUT

- How are your emotions and your behaviors connected? Have you always been aware of the connection, or are you learning something new about yourself?
- Is your behavioral style a reactive or a thoughtful response to your emotions? Is your behavioral style helping, hindering, or hurting you?

The Power of Self-Expression

If emotions are one side of being human, then thinking is the other. Whereas emotions are experienced as nonverbal sensations within us, thoughts are experienced in words. They give shape to our feelings and provide a language so that we can understand and better explore them.

Self-expression doesn't change the world—problems don't disappear because you wrote about them—but it does change you.

When you express yourself, you allow your thoughts and feelings to be used as allies, not as saboteurs of your life (and the lives of others). By expressing your feelings, you don't eliminate them but instead put them out into the world where you can see and manage them and ensure that they do no harm. Self-expression doesn't change the world—problems don't disappear because you wrote about them—but it does change *you*.

A Daily Journal

Writing helps. Even a few words each day can help unload thoughts and feelings, and put your day into perspective. The next journal entry provides a format for a daily journal entry. This is a simple entry that you can use to unload your thoughts and feelings, describe your day, and record what you're going through as part of your personal history. At the end of the entry add a thought for the day—something that impresses or inspires you or in some way is worth remembering. Finding a thought for each day pushes you to look outside of yourself, even as you find ways to express what's inside.

A DAILY DIARY

"When I write down my thoughts, they do not escape me.
This action makes me remember my strength."
— ISIDORE DUCASSE

Day: _____ Date: _____

1. What were the most pressing issues on your mind today?

_____

_____

_____

_____

2. What special tasks, events, or incidents stand out?

_____

_____

_____

_____

3. What did you accomplish today?

_____

_____

_____

_____

4. In general, how were you affected by this day?

_____

_____

_____

5. What's changing over time? Are the days getting easier or harder? More hopeful or less hopeful? Are issues getting resolved or building up?

_____

_____

_____

_____

6. What's going right?

_____

_____

_____

_____

7. *Today I'm feeling . . .* _____

_____

_____

_____

_____

8. *I want/need to say . . .* _____

_____

_____

_____

_____

9. Note any other reflections on the day or this time in your life.

_____

_____

_____

_____

_____

Thought for the day

_____

_____

_____

_____

_____

THINGS TO THINK ABOUT

- Are there especially difficult days ahead? If so, how can you best prepare for them, and what support do you need?
- Are the days going well? What can you do to improve the chances that they'll keep improving?
- Are there things pressing on you that need your attention? What will happen if they don't get your attention?

IO

Destination:
THE PAST—UNDERSTANDING
PERSONAL HISTORY

JAMES

My family was the perfect middle-class family, and I had a great up-bringing. There was no abuse or neglect in my life, I was never deprived of things I needed or wanted, and I recall a pretty good childhood. I was successful and well liked in high school, and college was a great experience. I just couldn't point back to an awful childhood, traumatic experience in adolescence, or major difficulties to explain away my addiction.

It wasn't until after I started counseling that I began to more closely look at the relationships of my earlier years and the expectations and roles that often came with those relationships. I started seeing the pressures to behave one way and not another, the directions I got steered into by family and friends, and the choices I made as the starting point to behaviors that only later flared up into addiction. I realized I'd never really thought about what I really wanted in those days and beyond. I'd hidden my disappointments from everyone's view, including my own, and instead lived my life by a pretty rigid set of

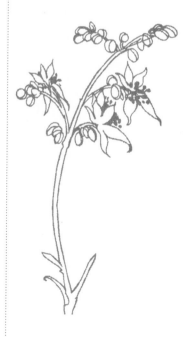

rules that, in the end, didn't work for me. Learning all this didn't change a thing about my present life, except it changed the way I came to see myself. And that was what helped me change my life.

IT HAS BECOME commonplace to observe that the past is prologue, that those who forget the past are bound to relive it. Author Salman Rushdie has said, "Our lives teach us who we are." Who we are today is an outgrowth of who we once were and what we experienced, and who we will become is an extension of who we are today. One way to come to know yourself is through your past—those shaping events and people who partly helped define the person you are today.

One way to come to know yourself is through your past— those shaping events and people who partly helped define the person you are today.

Imprints of the Family

Every family leaves its mark on its members. Family memories for some are wonderful reminiscences. For others, family life was chaotic, empty, or abusive, leaving painful memories.

Many dependencies and addictions are based on patterns that began to develop during adolescence or early adulthood. We can often discern similar patterns of behavior or addictions in grandparents, parents, or other family members.

Use the next journal entry to think about your immediate family and the features, attitudes, values, and behaviors you may share in common with them. Focus the entry on your parents, grandparents, older siblings, or other members of your family who were important in your life as you grew into early adulthood. Of course, not everyone grew up in a two-parent family. The point is to think about the family environment in which you grew up and the impact of that environment on you. Although the journal entry provides space for only one father and one mother, feel free to change these headings so that they describe your particular family.

FAMILY LIKENESSES

1. Briefly describe the family in which you grew up.

_____

_____

_____

_____

_____

_____

_____

2. What were the five things you most liked and most disliked about your family while growing up?

	Liked	*Disliked*
a.	_____	_____
b.	_____	_____
c.	_____	_____
d.	_____	_____
e.	_____	_____

3. What five things did you—or do you—like and dislike the most about your parents?

	Father		**Mother**	
	Like	*Dislike*	*Like*	*Dislike*
a.	_____	_____	_____	_____
b.	_____	_____	_____	_____
c.	_____	_____	_____	_____
d.	_____	_____	_____	_____
e.	_____	_____	_____	_____

4. List five ways you are similar to and dissimilar from your parents.

	Father		Mother	
	Similar	Dissimilar	Similar	Dissimilar
a.	_____	_____	_____	_____
b.	_____	_____	_____	_____
c.	_____	_____	_____	_____
d.	_____	_____	_____	_____
e.	_____	_____	_____	_____

5. List six attitudes, values, beliefs, or behaviors that you have acquired as a direct or indirect result of being a member of your family.

a. _____   d. _____

b. _____   e. _____

c. _____   f. _____

6. How did growing up in your family shape the person you are today?

_____

_____

_____

_____

_____

_____

_____

_____

THINGS TO THINK ABOUT

- Do you "look" like anyone in your family? Do your behaviors or relationships resemble those of a parent figure or sibling? If not, why not? If so, are these flattering resemblances or not?
- Do you *want* to emotionally and behaviorally look like anyone in your family?

Looking in the Mirror

Looking at yourself is like looking at a mirror image of your family. Just as people don't always like what they see when they look in a mirror, neither do they always like what they see in their own families. However, understanding your family is an important way to understand your own life. In some cases you may find that you haven't lived up to their finest qualities, or you may find that you've acquired some of their worst traits. Accepting that you share some of the qualities you most disliked in your parents can be painful.

Looking at yourself is like looking at a mirror image of your family.

People who are generally pleased and satisfied with their lives will find many positive traits learned from or shared with a parent or other important family members. However, addictive behaviors may also find their roots in the life of the family.

Use the next entry to focus on both your immediate and extended family (aunts, uncles, and cousins, for instance). Think carefully about each question before answering.

FAMILY INVENTORY

1. List five family members who were important to you growing up or in your adolescence. Next to each, write three to five adjectives describing those qualities that drew you to that person.

Important Family Member	Key Words
a. _____	_____
b. _____	_____
c. _____	_____
d. _____	_____
e. _____	_____

2. In what ways have you incorporated the best qualities of these important people into your own life?

_____

_____

_____

_____

3. In what ways have you incorporated the worst qualities of these important people into your own life?

_____

_____

_____

_____

4. Describe five family members who were unimportant to you growing up or in your adolescence. Next to each, write three to five words describing those qualities that distanced you from that person.

Unimportant Family Member	*Key Words*
a. _____	_____
b. _____	_____
c. _____	_____
d. _____	_____
e. _____	_____

5. In what ways have you become like these unimportant people?

_____

_____

_____

_____

6. What made the important people important?

_____

_____

_____

_____

_____

7. What made the unimportant relatives unimportant?

_____

_____

_____

_____

_____

8. What have you learned about yourself from your family, including both important and unimportant family members?

_____

_____

_____

_____

_____

_____

THINGS TO THINK ABOUT

- As you look at the family in which you grew up, do you see any of the roots of addiction?
- Have you built the most positive or most negative aspects of your early family life into your current life? Do your relationships today mirror the best or the worst of the family in which you grew up?

Addictive Families

In their book *Facing Shame,* Merle A. Fossum and Marilyn J. Mason suggest that addictive families share several related characteristics, and they describe eight "rules" they observed:

1. *Control.* Be in control of all behavior and interactions.

2. *Perfection.* Always be right and always do the right thing.

3. *Blame.* Blame others when things don't happen as planned.

4. *Denial.* Deny feelings, especially negative or vulnerable feelings.

5. *Unreliability.* Don't expect reliability or constancy in relationships.

6. *Incompleteness.* Don't bring transactions to completion or resolution.

7. *No talk.* Don't talk openly or directly about shameful, abusive, or compulsive behavior.

8. *Disqualification.* Discount, deny, or disguise shameful, abusive, or compulsive behavior.

An important part of overcoming your addiction means . . . working to . . . create new and healthy "rules" to live by.

As most of us carry the imprints of our family, many people with dependencies and addictions will continue to live by these rules, even if they're not always aware of them. An important part of overcoming your addiction means recognizing these eight behaviors and working to change them as you create new and healthy "rules" to live by.

The next journal entry will help you think about whether the family you grew up in lived by any or all of these rules and if you live by any of them now.

FAMILY RULES

1. Identify an earlier time in your life when you and your family behaved in a way consistent with Fossum and Mason's rules.

a. Control

Your family: _____

_____

You: _____

_____

b. Perfection

Your family: _____

_____

You: _____

_____

c. Blame

Your family: _____

_____

You: _____

_____

d. Denial

Your family: _____

_____

You: _____

_____

e. Unreliability

Your family: _____

_____

You: _____

_____

f. Incompleteness

Your family: _____

_____

You: _____

_____

g. No talk

Your family: _____

_____

You: _____

_____

h. Disqualification

Your family: _____

_____

You: _____

_____

2. Name a time in your *recent* history when you followed Fossum and Mason's rules.

a. Control: _____

_____

b. Perfection: _____

_____

c. Blame: _____

_____

d. Denial: _____

_____

e. Unreliability: _____

_____

f. Incompleteness: _____

_____

g. No talk: _____

_____

h. Disqualification: _____

_____

3. How has your addiction been affected or shaped by these rules?

_____

_____

_____

_____

4. Are you living your life today by these rules?

_____

_____

_____

5. Think of alternative rules to follow, and complete these sentences.

a. *Instead of control* . . . _____

_____

b. *Instead of perfection* . . . _____

_____

c. *Instead of blame* . . . _____

_____

d. *Instead of denial* . . . _____

_____

e. *Instead of unreliability* . . . _____

_____

f. *Instead of incompleteness* . . . _____

_____

g. *Instead of no talk* . . . _____

_____

h. *Instead of disqualification* . . . _____

_____

6. Can you live your life under these different rules? If not, what stops you?

_____

_____

_____

_____

7. Try to follow some of your new, alternative rules. Then complete the sentences, describing when you acted differently.

a. *Instead of acting under the* control *rule, I* . . . _____

_____

_____

b. *Instead of acting under the* perfection *rule, I* . . . _____

_____

_____

c. *Instead of acting under the* blame *rule, I* . . . _____

_____

_____

d. *Instead of acting under the* denial *rule, I* . . . _____

_____

_____

e. *Instead of acting under the* unreliability *rule, I . . .* _____

_____

f. *Instead of acting under the* incompleteness *rule, I . . .* _____

_____

g. *Instead of acting under the* no talk *rule, I . . .* _____

_____

h. *Instead of acting under the* disqualification *rule, I . . .* _____

_____

8. What was it like living and behaving under new rules?

_____

_____

_____

_____

_____

_____

_____

THINGS TO THINK ABOUT

- Do you live by rules? Are they healthy rules? Do these old rules apply to the way you normally act and interact with others?
- Were you able to create and test out new "rules" to live by? Should you find new rules to live by?

Family members often get locked into rigid roles. . . . Although at times these roles may be functional, they can also be both painful and destructive, especially if these are the only *roles a family member feels he or she can play.*

All the World's a Stage

In addictive families, family members often get locked into rigid roles, which might include the family hero, clown, scapegoat, black sheep, caretaker, or peacemaker. Although at times these roles may be functional, they can also be both painful and destructive, especially if these are the *only* roles a family member feels he or she can play. Under such circumstances, people can become unidimensional, their entire being and personality compressed into a single role. They fail to experiment or learn about different parts of themselves, and they face a pressure to conform to the expectations of other family members and friends, spouses, acquaintances, and bosses, too.

Use the next journal to explore the roles you play.

THE ROLE OF A LIFETIME

1. Is there a role you have been locked into since childhood, adolescence, or early adulthood? If not, what role do you *predominately* play in your current life?

_____

_____

_____

2. What are the rules that your role dictates? Add others below.

___blame   ___denial   ___incompleteness   ___perfection

___control   ___disqualification   ___no talk   ___unreliability

other: _____   _____

_____   _____

3. Can you step out of that role?

_____

_____

_____

4. What might happen if you did step out of the role?

_____

_____

_____

_____

_____

_____

5. Try stepping out of your role for forty-eight hours. If you are a hero, spend forty-eight hours allowing yourself to feel scared or overwhelmed or to ask someone else for help. If you're a peacemaker, let others fight it out. Continue this entry after you've completed this two-day exercise.

6. Were you able to step out of the role? If so, what did it feel like? If not, what prevented you?

_____

_____

_____

_____

_____

_____

_____

7. What have you learned about the role or roles you play?

_____

_____

_____

_____

_____

_____

8. How do these roles help, hinder, or hurt you?

_____

_____

_____

_____

THINGS TO THINK ABOUT

- Are you stuck in only one or two roles? Are you fulfilled by the roles you play, or do you feel held back?
- Are the roles you play roles you learned in the family you grew up in, or are they new roles you've learned to play since? Either way, are they *healthy* roles?
- Is it important to learn or play new roles?

The Roots of Addiction

Memories, good and bad, remind us of events around which our lives have turned. They are part of the foundation on which our current lives are built.

Why do some people become addicted and not others? Is there such a thing as an addictive personality? Is addiction biological in nature, or is it the result of the environment you grew up in or live in today? Opinions differ. We do not know for certain the answers at this time. However, the *roots* of your addiction lie somewhere in your past.

Think now about your past. What stands out for you? What moments are frozen in time? Sometimes these moments are remembered with great pleasure or joy, such as an award, the beginning of a valued relationship, or a day. Sometimes the moment stands out as a clear turning point or change in direction, such as a decision to marry or a career choice. Not all moments are remembered with pleasure; some are tinged with sorrow, anger, or fear. Memories, good and bad, remind us of events around which our lives have turned. They are part of the foundation on which our current lives are built.

Use the next journal entry to think about important moments and events in your life. Consider moments that stand out in your mind as helping to shape who you became and who you are. Think especially about those moments during which your addiction was forged and those moments that have given you the strength and fortitude to remain in recovery and overcome your addiction.

LIFE MARKERS: DEFINING MOMENTS

1. Describe three important moments that affected or shaped your life during the following times.

a. Childhood: _____

_____

_____

b. Adolescence: _____

_____

_____

c. Early adulthood: _____

_____

_____

2. Describe three important *recent* moments that have affected or reshaped your life.

a. _____

b. _____

c. _____

3. Describe one of the painful or disappointing moments of your life.

_____

_____

_____

4. Describe one of the positive and most affirming moments of your life.

_____

_____

_____

5. How have these defining moments and experiences come together to shape the person you are today?

_____

_____

_____

_____

_____

_____

6. How have these moments contributed to the development of your addiction?

_____

_____

_____

_____

_____

7. How can you draw strength from what these defining moments have taught or given to you?

_____

_____

_____

_____

_____

THINGS TO THINK ABOUT

- Is your history connected to your present? Can you find the roots of your addiction in past experiences or relationships?
- Can you use your history as a tool to guide you in the right direction? Can you use your history to find strength and direction?

Landmark Relationships

Just as there are defining moments in your life, so too are there individuals who, intentionally or otherwise, helped define your thinking, personality, and life. These are landmark relationships because they defined your life in some significant way and made a meaningful contribution to who you became. Just because you've known someone all your life doesn't necessarily indicate a significant or landmark relationship. Perhaps it's the relationship that *didn't* happen that holds special meaning for you, or maybe it's a grade school teacher whom you haven't seen for twenty years who continues to shape your life.

The next entry will help you think about important people and relationships.

Just as there are defining moments in your life, so too are there individuals who, intentionally or otherwise, helped define your thinking, personality, and life.

LIFE MARKERS: PEOPLE

1. List five people who have been or still are important in your life, and why:

Person	Importance of This Person or Relationship
a. _____	_____
b. _____	_____
c. _____	_____
d. _____	_____
e. _____	_____

2. What did each person or relationship offer you?

a. _____

b. _____

c. _____

d. _____

e. _____

3. How did each person or relationship affect or shape your life *then*?

a. _____

b. _____

c. _____

d. _____

e. _____

4. How did each person or relationship influence the person you are *today*?

a. _____

b. _____

c. _____

d. _____

e. _____

5. How have these people and relationships together contributed to help build the person you are today?

_____

_____

_____

_____

_____

_____

_____

6. What can you draw most from these important relationships that can help you define for yourself the kind of person you *want* to be today?

_____

_____

_____

_____

THINGS TO THINK ABOUT

- Do important people come to mind easily, or is it difficult to get in touch with who most influenced your development?
- Are your memories of important people sweet, bittersweet, or difficult? Is there a pattern of some kind evident in the relationships that most affected and influenced your development?
- Of the people whom you've identified as important, who do you *most* want to be like? Why? Who do you *least* want to be like? Why?

Past Loss

Losses can include lost relationships, marriages, children, jobs, homes, health, finances, opportunities, the trust of others, dreams, and self-esteem. In Chapter 5 you completed an inventory of your losses. Losses that remain unprocessed, or unresolved, are a frequent cause of relapse. In such a situation, the emotional pain or wounds from the loss have never been fully dealt with, leaving a emotional gap filled in some way by the addiction. In recovery the numbing effect of addiction wears off, allowing the pain of loss to reappear.

Losses that remain unprocessed, or unresolved, are a frequent cause of relapse.

Review the journal entry An Inventory of Losses on page 82 and ask whether each has been worked through or remains a source of pain and discomfort. Then complete the next entry.

LOST INNOCENCE

1. What stand out as your greatest losses?

_____

_____

_____

_____

_____

_____

2. How have these losses helped shape your life today?

_____

_____

_____

_____

_____

3. How have these losses helped shape your behaviors today?

_____

_____

_____

_____

_____

4. What past losses have been left unresolved?

_____

_____

_____

_____

_____

5. What past pain continues to affect you today?

_____

_____

_____

_____

_____

6. Has loss contributed to the maintenance of your addictions? Explain.

_____

_____

_____

_____

_____

THINGS TO THINK ABOUT

- Is there a relationship between loss and your addiction? Is there a relationship between *unresolved* loss and your addiction?
- Is it important to try to resolve prior losses and trauma? If so, what help do you need, or who can you turn to for help?

Tomorrow's Past

Understanding the past is not a cure-all. Nothing changes simply because you've learned about what makes you tick. Bad relationships remain bad, problems don't go away, and bad habits still plague you. But understanding your past offers clues into *why* you might behave the way you do and how those behaviors developed. Tomorrow is built on today.

Tomorrow is built on today.

11

Destination:
SELF-INVENTORY

NANCY

My addiction was so out of control that it fooled me. I stopped seeing, or maybe never saw, how my gambling affected everyone else around me. I didn't realize how driven and selfish I'd become and how unimportant everyone else had become in turn. I took the lies I told for granted and even came to believe some of them. I found lots of ways to justify what I was doing and what I thought I needed, and I found many ways to switch off my conscience. The fact that I was driving my husband and kids into ruin somehow slipped my notice. It took bankruptcy and court-ordered counseling for me to actually see myself for the first time in many years.

CATHERINE

It was only after I looked hard at myself and completed a self-inventory that my life really started to change. I realized how hard I'd become, and uncaring. I hated what I saw and cried about it on and off for days. I was still a good person, yet I realized I was also dishonest, critical of everyone else, focused on meeting my own needs above the needs of others, and driven by a need to feel better

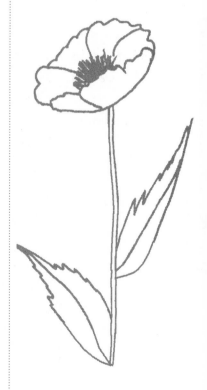

about who I was. I didn't like my inventory as all. But it, most of all, was the turning point in beating my addiction.

THE AA MODEL and other similar recovery programs require as one of their steps a "searching and fearless moral inventory of ourselves." Recovery involves more than just support, willpower, and techniques for maintaining abstinence or moderation. It also requires a permanent change in perspective and lifestyle that can only come from increased insight and self-awareness. This chapter will provide you with an opportunity to take stock of your life and make that "searching and fearless moral inventory."

Recovery involves more than just support, willpower, and techniques for maintaining abstinence or moderation. It also requires a permanent change in perspective and lifestyle that can only come from increased insight and self-awareness.

Facing Strengths and Weaknesses

We all have our weak points as well as strengths. Taking inventory means taking an honest look at both. As you learn more about your strengths, you'll increase your ability to call on them as you enter and remain in lifetime recovery. By exploring your weaknesses, you'll be better equipped to face and overcome them.

A Searching and Fearless Moral Inventory

Facing up to your weaknesses is a difficult matter. Eighteenth-century French philosopher Jean-Jacques Rousseau observed that "nature never deceives us; it is we who deceive ourselves." Accordingly, you must be *fearless* when taking stock of those aspects of your personality and behavior that you might prefer to avoid thinking about. A *moral* inventory requires that you examine your behaviors and interactions in terms of right and wrong by taking into accounts the costs of and damage caused by your addiction. Moral attitudes and behaviors are those that are principled, uncorrupted, and honorable. Only you can decide what is a moral weakness, but when coupled with a *fearless* commitment to learning the truth and honestly taking stock of your life, you'll know what's right and what's wrong when you see it. Finally, if you're prepared to take fearless and moral stock, you must be willing to continue searching, despite the emotional discomfort you may encounter.

Because taking inventory will set the pace for the work ahead—making permanent change, restoring relationships, and rebuilding your life—do not continue with the next journal entry until you are committed to learning the truth about yourself.

STRENGTHS AND FLAWS

1. List your five greatest strengths and your five greatest flaws

Strength	Flaw
a. _____	_____
b. _____	_____
c. _____	_____
d. _____	_____
e. _____	_____

2. List three people you trust to be honest with you.

a. _____

b. _____

c. _____

3. Ask each person you listed to write down and give to you what they consider to be your five greatest strengths and your five greatest flaws. Do their lists match your own, or are they considerably different? Do their lists match one another's?

_____

_____

_____

_____

4. What can you learn about your strengths and flaws based on your friends' lists?

_____

_____

_____

_____

_____

5. What can you learn about the way people see you based on their lists?

_____

_____

_____

_____

_____

6. If your list is significantly different from their lists, what does this tell you about the way you see yourself? If your list is similar, what does this say?

_____

_____

_____

_____

_____

7. Make a new list of personal strengths and flaws that combines all lists.

Strength	*Flaw*
a. _____	_____
b. _____	_____
c. _____	_____
d. _____	_____
e. _____	_____

8. Are there things you can do to maximize the positive effects of your strengths and minimize the damage caused by your flaws? Explain.

_____

_____

_____

_____

_____

_____

THINGS TO THINK ABOUT

- Do you have three people you trust well enough to ask for an assessment of your strengths and flaws? If not, what does this say about your relationships or the way you've chosen to live your life? If so, were you able to honestly accept their assessment of you?
- Could you list five strengths? Could you list five flaws? Was it difficult to think about your flaws?

Attitudes and Interactions

People with addictions often develop attitudes and behaviors that support their addiction. However, sometimes these attitudes are already in place prior to becoming addicted and help pave the way for, and eventually maintain, addiction. Although no direct relationship has been established between these attitudes and addiction, because of their inherently antisocial nature they insulate you from interacting with people and things in the world around you.

Use the next journal entry to take a hard look at your attitudes and behaviors, especially those that may be antisocial, self-defeating, or harmful. These are the attitudes and behaviors to become aware of and change.

People with addictions often develop attitudes and behaviors that support their addiction. However, sometimes these attitudes are already in place prior to becoming addicted and help pave the way for, and eventually maintain, addiction.

THE WORST OF ME

1. Check off every attitude or behavior that matches the way you feel about yourself, other people, or the way you see and interact with the world. Next to each attitude or behavior you check off, complete the sentence to describe how you live out this anti-social, self-defeating, or harmful attitude or behavior.

__abusive   I . . . _____

__angry   I . . . _____

__arrogant   I . . . _____

__bitter   I . . . _____

__cheating   I . . . _____

__controlling   I . . . _____

__cynical   I . . . _____

__deceitful   I . . . _____

__dishonest   I . . . _____

__dominating   I . . . _____

__egotistical   I . . . _____

__entitled   I . . . _____

__grandiose   I . . . _____

__greedy   I . . . _____

__intolerant   I . . . _____

__irresponsible   I . . . _____

__jealous   I . . . _____

__manipulative   I . . . _____

__neglectful   I . . . _____

__prejudiced   I . . . _____

__prideful   I . . . _____

__procrastinating   I . . . _____

___resentful   I... _____

___sarcastic   I... _____

___secretive   I... _____

___self-indulgent   I... _____

___selfish   I... _____

___self-pitying   I... _____

___unappreciative   I... _____

___uncaring   I... _____

___unconcerned   I... _____

___unethical   I... _____

___unforgiving   I... _____

___ungrateful   I... _____

___unlistening   I... _____

___unresponsive   I... _____

___untrusting   I... _____

___vain   I... _____

___vengeful   I... _____

other: _____   I... _____

_____   I... _____

_____   I... _____

_____   I... _____

_____   I... _____

_____   I... _____

2. Of the attitudes and behaviors you checked off, which are the five most antisocial, self-defeating, or harmful, and why?

a. _____ because _____

_____

b. _____ because _____

_____

c. _____ because _____

_____

d. _____ because _____

_____

e. _____ because _____

_____

3. How are you most damaged by negative attitudes or behaviors?

_____

_____

_____

_____

_____

4. How are the people closest to you harmed by these attitudes and behaviors?

_____

_____

_____

_____

_____

5. How are other relationships most harmed by these attitudes and behaviors?

_____

_____

_____

_____

_____

6. How can you best use your strengths to challenge and change negative attitudes and behaviors?

_____

_____

_____

_____

_____

7. What most needs to change about your attitude?

_____

_____

_____

_____

_____

8. What most needs to change about your behavior?

_____

_____

_____

_____

_____

THINGS TO THINK ABOUT

- Is it difficult to take stock of your flaws?
- Do you think that these sort of attitudes and behaviors are related to your addiction? Do they need to change? Do you have the strength to change them? Do you need help to change them?
- Can you show or discuss this list with others and get their input? If not, why not? If so, what is it about those people that makes them safe?

Judgments and Acceptance

Many people with addictions have unrealistically high expectations. They constantly judge both themselves and others, which not only makes it hard for them to get support from others but also increases the feelings of shame that can contribute to addiction. One important part of recovery is learning acceptance of both yourself and others.

Many people with addictions have unrealistically high expectations.

Use the next journal entry to explore judgment or, more to the point, *not* passing judgment. Spend one full day without passing any judgments. Don't judge anyone or anything. Don't say or think "That was a boring movie," "That's an ugly color," "I wouldn't be caught dead in an outfit like that," "This is the stupidest thing I've ever done," or even "This is the most useful self-help book I've ever used." *Note:* For the purposes of this exercise, judgment refers to the way that we assess and evaluate the people and things in our life as good or bad, useful or not useful, worthwhile or not worthwhile. This is *not* the same as the judgments, decisions, and evaluations required to successfully negotiate everyday life. For example, your job may require you to make decisions based on judgments, and you may have to routinely judge how to best handle any given relationship or situation. For the No-Judgment Day entry that follows the goal is to not pass judgments about intrinsic worth and even to avoid judgments of any kind *when you can.*

Use a notebook to keep track of every time you make a judgment. Do this for seven days *or* until you successfully pass an entire day without making any judgments at all. Complete the next journal entry at the end of the seven days *or* as soon as you've completed one full day without making any judgments.

NO-JUDGMENT DAY

1. Were you able to pass one full day without making any judgments?

_____

2. During your first day, how much time passed before you made your first judgment?

_____

3. Were you able to easily catch yourself making judgments? Why or why not?

_____

_____

_____

4. How many judgments did you typically make each day?

_____

5. How much time typically passed between judgments? Did you make judgments every few minutes or only once a day?

_____

_____

_____

6. Did you tend to judge yourself or other people more? Explain.

_____

_____

_____

7. Were there any patterns to the sort of judgments you made? For example, did your judgments tend to be more positive than negative? Did you find that there's one area you tend to be more judgmental about than others? Describe the patterns your judgments took.

_____

_____

_____

8. Were there any factors that affected the type or frequency of judgments you made? For instance, were you more judgmental at the start or end of the day? Did stressful interactions with people affect the judgments you made? Describe the patterns your judgments took.

_____

_____

_____

9. What did being *non*judgmental teach you about being judgmental?

_____

_____

_____

_____

THINGS TO THINK ABOUT

- Are you a judgmental person? If so, do your judgments of others and yourself hurt you in some way?
- How does your pattern of judgment passing affect your expectations of yourself and others? How do these expectations contribute to your addiction?
- Is it important to learn to be more nonjudgmental?

Shame

Feelings of shame can feed addiction.

Feelings of shame can feed addiction. Shame often results in keeping things secret. Remember from Chapter 10 that two of the rules an addictive family keeps are secrecy (not talking openly or directly about shameful, abusive, or compulsive behavior) and hiding (denying or disguising shameful, abusive, or compulsive behavior).

Are there things in your life that have happened to you or that you have done to yourself or others that you're ashamed of and have kept secret? Are there patterns of behaviors or thoughts you have that you are too embarrassed by to reveal to anyone else? Are you filled with shame about your addiction itself or the fact that you haven't been able to overcome it? Do you feel the need to maintain a facade behind which the "real" you exists? Do you lie about yourself to others and yourself? If shame and secrets are getting in the way of how you interact with the world, then they're problems you must overcome.

Use the next journal entry to think about experiences, behaviors, thoughts, or feelings that fill you with shame or embarrassment, that have led to secrets and perhaps even lies, that you must grapple with to continue your *fearless* inventory.

THE SHAMEFUL TRUTH

"[We] both conceal and disguise ourselves from ourselves."
—W. F. TROTTER

1. Describe three things that shame or embarrass you, that no one knows about you.

a. The secret: _____

What is shaming about this secret? _____

_____

What do you fear will happen if people learn of this secret? _____

_____

_____

In what way does keeping this secret affect your life? _____

_____

_____

_____

b. The secret: _____

What is shaming about this secret? _____

_____

What do you fear will happen if people learn of this secret? _____

_____

_____

In what way does keeping this secret affect your life? _____

_____

_____

_____

c. The secret: _____

What is shaming about this secret? _____

_____

What do you fear will happen if people learn of this secret? _____

_____

_____

In what way does keeping this secret affect your life? _____

_____

_____

_____

2. Is there anyone you trust enough to share one of these secrets with? If not, skip to Question 3. If so, complete these sentences. Then continue with Question 4.

a. *The secret I am willing to risk sharing with someone is . . .* _____

_____

b. *If I share this secret, I'm afraid that . . .* _____

_____

_____

_____

c. *The way I feel about myself when I think about this secret is . . .* _____

_____

_____

3. If you don't feel able or willing to share a secret, complete these sentences.

a. *I'm not willing to disclose secrets to other people because . . .* _____

_____

_____

b. *If I share a secret, I'm afraid that . . .* _____

_____

_____

c. *The way I feel about myself when I think about my secrets is . . .* _____

_____

_____

d. What most prevents you from sharing or disclosing your secrets?

_____

_____

_____

4. How does shame hold you back?

_____

_____

_____

_____

5. How do secrets affect your life?

_____

_____

_____

_____

6. Do shame and secrets play into your addiction? If so, how?

_____

_____

_____

_____

_____

7. How are you feeling right now?

_____

_____

_____

_____

_____

THINGS TO THINK ABOUT

- Was it difficult to write down these secrets? Are you ashamed even to discuss them with yourself?
- Do you need to deal with shame and resolve secrets to improve and move on with your life? Can you restore, build, and maintain healthy relationships if you keep shame hidden?
- Are there people in your life with whom you can take risks? Are you willing to take a chance? Can you disclose secrets and shame to a therapist or counselor?

Taking a Chance

The last journal entry may have helped you make the decision to unburden yourself by sharing your secret shame with another person. Even if you're not ready to do this, it's important for you to keep thinking about disclosure and trust. The act of sharing something personal with someone can be cathartic. It unburdens you and lets it all out. It can also help you move on. You may discover that your secret was no big deal after all, or you may find that you must now take responsibility for resolving a situation that you've been hiding until now.

The act of sharing something personal with someone can be cathartic. It unburdens you and lets it all out.

Taking Stock

What have you learned about yourself through developing a self-inventory? Use this final entry to reflect on your work in this chapter. If you've had a difficult time with carrying out a "searching and fearless moral inventory," then you may need to do more work on this before moving on to the tasks and challenges of Stage 4. If you feel ready to move on, remember that your self-inventory isn't over just because you've finished this chapter. Maintaining self-awareness and honesty are lifetime tasks.

DOING RIGHT

1. Do you need to change your attitudes? If so, which ones?

_____

_____

_____

2. Do you need to change your behaviors? If so, which ones?

_____

_____

_____

3. Do you need to change the way you think? If so, in what ways?

_____

_____

_____

4. Do you need to be less deceitful and more honest with people? If so, in what ways and with whom?

_____

_____

_____

5. Do you need to start trusting other people more?

_____

_____

_____

6. Do you need to find more people you can trust?

_____

_____

_____

7. Do you owe anyone the truth?

_____

_____

_____

8. Do you owe anyone apologies?

_____

_____

_____

THINGS TO THINK ABOUT

- Have you really been honest with yourself in this chapter? Are you ready to go on, or do you need to work more on your self-inventory?
- Are you ready to tackle the real process of change that lies ahead? What sort of changes are you expecting? What sort of help and support do you need?

12

*"The ideal is in thyself,
the impediment too is in
thyself."*
——THOMAS CARLYLE

Destination:
SELF-ESTEEM AND PERSONAL IDENTITY

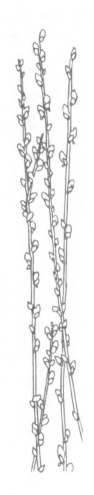

BENNY

I'd disappointed so many people for so long that I'd built it into my identity. I was a failure. Not only would I never succeed, but drinking helped make me feel better about being a failure. So the cure for my failure was also the thing that kept me failing and feeling like a failure. Whew!

MAC

I had to start seeing myself differently before I could start doing things differently. That was tough. My self-image was a long time forming, and developing a different one wasn't something that I could do overnight. First I had to understand the way I saw myself when I was using and the way I'd come to see and feel about myself for so many years (going back to being a teenager, actually). Then I had to picture the identity I wanted to have. I forged a new identity out of the fire of my addiction.

MORE THAN ANYTHING else, the way that addicts *think* and *feel* about themselves and the world is what fuels their addiction. Accordingly, to effect recovery, addicts must change their perspective.

A strong sense of personal identity is intrinsic to *any* success in life (however you define success). People are far more likely to feel successful if they experience themselves as powerful, capable, adequate, and authentic rather than weak, incapable, unworthy, and artificial. In the last chapter you spent time exploring your strengths and weaknesses, making a critical assessment of your attitudes, values, behaviors, and general view of the world. This chapter will help you focus specifically on self-esteem and the development of a personal identity that is oriented to success rather than addiction.

> *More than anything else, the way that addicts* think *and* feel *about themselves and the world is what fuels their addiction.*

Positive Self-Regard

The way you experience yourself is related to your actions and the results produced by those actions. If what you do repeatedly leads to failed endeavors, unsatisfying relationships, and disappointment in general, you will not develop a healthy self-image. By contrast, people who do things that lead to desired and positive outcomes stand a far greater chance of feeling good about themselves and their ability to lead the life they want to lead. Ultimately, your goal should be to behave in ways that are personally fulfilling, lead to a sense of accomplishment and satisfaction, and help you feel better about yourself.

Self-Concept

The terms *self-esteem* and *self-image* usually refer to a complex interrelationship among three different aspects of self-concept.

1. Self-esteem equals self-worth, or how you *feel* about your-self. People with high self-esteem have personal regard and generally feel pretty good about themselves. High self-esteem helps people tolerate difficult times and face lack of success without emotionally crumbling. People with low self-esteem tend to feel bad about themselves; some even say they don't like themselves.

2. Self-image is a reflection of how you *see* yourself. People with a positive self-image think of themselves as reasonably effective and capable and as someone others would want to know. On the other hand, people with a negative self-image see themselves as incapable and sometimes undesirable.

3. Personal identity reflects *who* you are, or the way you view your role in the world and your relationships with others. Your sense of identity is built on the things you do, your impact on the world, and your perception of your value to others. People with poorly defined identities often are con-fused about what's important to them, their personal rela-tionships, and the value to others of the things they do.

Personal identity reflects who you are, or the way you view your role in the world and your relationships with others.

Problems with Self-Concept

Low self-esteem, negative self-image, and confused personal iden-tity are serious problems. A negative or uncertain sense of self, accompanied by feelings of incompetence, inadequacy, or help-lessness, result in emotional problems and an impaired ability to function effectively. On the other hand, positive self-regard con-tributes to a sense of empowerment. You feel good, *capable,* and determined to behave productively. Of course a clearly defined personal identity and high self-regard don't guarantee success, but positive self-regard allows you to weather failure, withstand self-doubt, and take things in stride without your self-image crumbling.

Use the next journal entry to assess the way you see yourself. Keep in mind that self-esteem, self-image, and personal identity change over time, especially during recovery, so you may wish to check in with yourself periodically.

WHEN I THINK OF MYSELF . . .

1. Self-Esteem

a. On this 1 to 5 scale, circle the number that most approximates your sense of self-regard.

Low Self-Esteem:	High Self-Esteem:
I really feel bad about myself.	*I really feel good about myself.*

    1   2   3   4   5

b. Explain your rating. How do you *feel* about yourself, and why?

_____

_____

_____

2. Self-Image

a. On this 1 to 5 scale, circle the number that most approximates your sense of self-image.

Negative Self-Image:	Positive Self-Image:
I see myself as really ineffective.	*I see myself as really effective.*

    1   2   3   4   5

b. Explain your answer. How do you *see* yourself, and why?

_____

_____

_____

3. Personal Identity

a. On this 1 to 5 scale, circle the number that most approximates your sense of personal identity.

Confused and Uncertain Identity:
I'm confused or uncertain about my role.

Clear and Certain Identity:
I'm clear and certain about my role.

I   2   3   4   5

b. Explain your answer. In what ways do you experience confusion or clarity about who you are as a person, both in terms of identity and role?

_____

_____

_____

_____

4. How much does your addiction affect the way you feel about yourself (your self-esteem)?

_____

_____

_____

_____

5. How much does your addiction influence the way you see yourself (your self-image)?

_____

_____

_____

_____

6. How much does your addiction define your place in society (your personal identity)?

_____

_____

_____

7. Describe your *overall* self-concept. How do you generally see yourself?

_____

_____

_____

_____

8. How much has addiction affected your overall self-concept?

_____

_____

_____

_____

9. What's changed the most in your self-concept since your addiction?

_____

_____

_____

_____

10. *When I think of myself, I . . .* _____

_____

_____

_____

THINGS TO THINK ABOUT

- How do you view yourself: strong or weak, effective or ineffective? Were you always this way, or did addiction change things?
- How important is self-concept in overcoming your addiction and moving forward? Can you succeed without a positive opinion of yourself? If not, how can you begin to build positive self-image?

Self-Defeating Thinking

People occasionally misinterpret or misunderstand things. This is normal. However, sometimes they develop a *pattern* of irrational thought that clouds their judgment and contributes to weak relationships and low self-esteem. Thoughts that are based on emotional misreasoning, irrational and unrealistic ideas, and misinformation are known as cognitive distortions, which interfere with healthy functioning, self-perception, and relationships (see Chapter 3). Cognitive distortions prevent people from responding to situations in a thoughtful manner. Instead, they respond in a knee-jerk fashion. This style of thinking hampers the development of self-esteem because it becomes part of a negative cycle in which a poor self-image is (a) built on incorrect assumptions about yourself or other people, which can lead to (b) a misinterpretation of the things that happen to you, which may trigger (c) knee-jerk reactions and behaviors, which have (d) unpleasant emotional or practical consequences, which lead back to (e) the sense that nothing ever goes right for you, by which (f) low self-esteem is confirmed and serves as the foundation on which poor self-image is built. This self-defeating cycle can only be interrupted by understanding how you respond to situations and learning how to change your irrational thought patterns into rational, realistic ones.

The next journal entry provides a means for exploring the ways in which your thinking may at times be irrational or distorted.

Thoughts that are based on emotional misreasoning, irrational and unrealistic ideas, and misinformation are known as cognitive distortions, which interfere with healthy functioning, self-perception, and relationships.

DISTORTIONS IN THINKING

1. Check off any of these irrational thinking styles that fit the way you think.

___ *Emotional misreasoning.* You draw an irrational and incorrect conclusion based on the way you feel at that moment. "I *feel* stupid, so I must *be* stupid."

___*Overgeneralization*. You reach an incorrect conclusion that has far-reaching implications based on a single experience or a small set of experiences. You assume that your experience in one situation is a reflection of the ways things are in all situations. "I failed to stay sober *this* week, so I'll *never* succeed in staying sober."

___*Catastrophic thinking*. You magnify the impact of negative experiences to extreme proportions. "If I have even *one* relapse, my *entire* sobriety will fall to pieces."

___*Black-and-white thinking*. You see things as all or nothing. "*Either* I'm a success in recovery *or* I'm a total failure."

___*Shoulds and musts*. You feel you *should* do something or that things *must* be a certain way. You feel that you absolutely must behave in a particular way or think that you should have a level of control over the world around you. "I *should* be able to conquer this addiction by sheer willpower. I *must* be able to do this on my own."

___*Negative predictions/fortune telling*. You predict failure in situations yet to happen because things have gone wrong before. "I've never been able to be disciplined *before,* and therefore I will *never* have self discipline."

___*Projection*. You make negative assumptions about the thoughts, intentions, or motives of another person, which are often projections of your own thought and feelings about the situation. "*He* knows I have a problem. *He* thinks it's my fault and that I'm a loser."

___*Mind reading*. You feel that others should know how you feel or what you want, even though you don't tell them. "She *should've known* that I need her support. I shouldn't have to tell her."

___*Labeling*. You label yourself or someone else in a simplistic, negative way, which shapes the way you see yourself or that other person. "Because I have an addiction, *I'm* a failure." "Because my wife doesn't understand my needs, *she's* no good at all."

___*Personalization*. You treat a negative event as a personal reflection or confirmation of your own worthlessness. "I couldn't hold that job because of my addiction. I knew it would go that way because I'm a failure, and this just proves it. Nothing ever goes right for me because I'm worthless."

___*Negative focus*. You focus mainly on negative events, memories, or implications while you ignore more neutral or positive information about yourself or a situation. "It *doesn't matter* that I have two children who care for and love me or that I have been successful in my marriage. I'm no good and a failure *because* I have an addiction I can't deal with."

__*Cognitive avoidance*. You avoid thinking about emotionally difficult subjects because they feel overwhelming or insurmountable. "I can't even *think* about it, let alone try to change it."

2. Are there other types of cognitive distortions that characterize your thinking?

_____

_____

_____

_____

3. If you identified any types of cognitive distortions, are they typical of the way you think, or do you tend to slip into irrational thinking only under certain conditions or times in your life?

_____

_____

_____

_____

4. Are these sort of thinking distortions affecting your self-esteem and self-image?

_____

_____

_____

_____

5. Are cognitive distortions influencing your behavior?

_____

_____

_____

_____

6. In what way have cognitive distortions shaped or fueled your addiction?

_____

_____

_____

_____

THINGS TO THINK ABOUT

- How can you tell when your thinking is distorted or irrational?
- How might cognitive distortions affect the course of your recovery?
- Can you think of recent situations in which you used cognitive distortions?

Self-Affirmation

Nothing builds success like success. A self-affirming cycle allows personal achievements to lay the groundwork for further accomplishment. These positive experiences are empowering and contribute to an overall healthy sense of self. Low self-esteem, negative self-image, and a confused personal identity, however, lead to a self-defeating cycle in which a single negative experience promotes other such experiences.

A self-affirming cycle allows personal achievements to lay the groundwork for further accomplishment.

These cycles are driven in part by the things you do and the relationships you have, but the "glue" that holds things together is perception, or the way you see things. People who distort their experiences so that everything is seen as a loss or confirmation of a dismal world will have a difficult time finding the good in anything, including themselves. On the other hand, a willingness to see the positive even under difficult circumstances provides the fuel for self-affirmation and can contribute to an improved sense of yourself and your capacity to survive difficult times and grow stronger as a result.

For every disappointment and failure in your life, there's almost certainly a satisfying and successful experience waiting to be counted. However, you have to be able to *see* those achievements in your history and daily life in order to count them as a measure of your success. Recognizing and praising yourself for your successes is one way to affirm your positive qualities. An affirmation is an assertion of a truth, a belief, or an ideal—a way to put out an idea and commit yourself to it. In this case, the affirmation reflects your commitment to *yourself*—your own health, goodness, strength, and ability to get through a difficult time in your life.

For every disappointment and failure in your life, there's almost certainly a satisfying and successful experience waiting to be counted.

Use the next journal entry to think about successes, small and large, in your life.

I AM . . .

1. List four things of which you're proud. These can include goals you've achieved, special skills, personal relationships, adversity you've overcome, decisions you've made, or a particular role you play in life.

a. _____

b. _____

c. _____

d. _____

2. List four personal qualities about which you feel good. These can include your generosity, the way you look, your sense of humor, being a good spouse or parent, your compassion for issues or empathy for others, your ability to make new friends, or your attitudes and beliefs.

a. _____

b. _____

c. _____

d. _____

3. Complete these sentences.

a. *I know I can deal with difficult times because I . . .* _____

_____

_____

b. *Even though there are always things to feel badly about, I . . .* _____

_____

_____

c. *Although my addiction has deeply affected my life, I . . .* _____

_____

_____

d. *I draw strength from . . .* _____

_____

_____

e. *Above all I value myself because . . .* _____

_____

_____

f. *One thought that helps me through difficult times is . . .* _____

_____

_____

THINGS TO THINK ABOUT

- Were you able to describe achievements or personal qualities of which you're proud? If not, do you need help figuring out how to feel better about yourself?
- Do self-reinforcing thoughts help you gather internal strength or feel better about yourself during a difficult time?

A Changing Identity

Recovering addicts often think about an addiction-free life without paying much attention to the powerful, central role the addiction once played in their lives and identity. However disorganized or chaotic life became, it was always focused on the addiction. Ending addiction and beginning recovery involves changing this focus and forging a new identity. This is accomplished in the following ways.

Disengagement is the process of separating from your addiction and from the way of life associated with it.

- *Disengagement* is the process of separating from your addiction and from the way of life associated with it.

- *Disidentification* is the process of changing the way you think about yourself and "disidentifying" from your former identity as an addict.

- *Disenchantment* is the process of discovering that the reality you believed in when you were addicted was an illusion. This disenchantment with your former life and beliefs is a crucial part of change.

- *Disorientation* is the process of reorganizing your life and finding your bearings in this new addiction-free world. When you were addicted, many aspects of your life were ordered and oriented by your addiction. When you give up your addiction, it is natural to feel disoriented and confused. You need a new compass and a new map.

Use the final entry in this chapter to solidify the end of your old identity and the beginning of your new one.

NEW HORIZONS

Disengagement

1. In giving up your addiction, what else in your former life are you separating from?

_____

_____

_____

_____

2. Describe the previous way of life from which you have disengaged.

_____

_____

_____

_____

Disidentification

3. How has giving up your addiction changed the way you think about yourself?

_____

_____

_____

_____

4. What were you before your disidentification?

_____

_____

_____

5. What are you now?

_____

_____

_____

Disenchantment

6. What have you learned about yourself and about life as a result of your disenchantment?

_____

_____

_____

_____

7. What was previously an illusion?

_____

_____

_____

_____

Disorientation

8. In what ways do you feel disoriented and confused without your addiction?

_____

_____

_____

_____

9. What assumptions have you given up in the process of giving up your addiction?

_____

_____

_____

10. Do you have a new map and compass?

_____

_____

_____

11. What is it like to give up your addiction?

_____

_____

_____

12. What will you most miss?

_____

_____

_____

13. What will you most gain?

_____

_____

_____

THINGS TO THINK ABOUT

- What *is* your new identity? How fragile is this new self-view? What must you do to maintain and develop your new identity?
- Have you really disengaged and disidentified from your identity as an addict?

13

Destination:

UNDERSTANDING

RELATIONSHIPS

TINA

My life was really shattered, but I didn't want to see it. I tried my best to live on the outer edge of my life and didn't want to look any deeper. I tried to pretend that things were okay with my family life, but it was harder and harder to ignore how mean and angry my husband was because of my gambling and how my youngest kid just dismissed me and treated me like a loser. I'd lost all respect at home, and that was affecting my self-respect. I knew, of course, that they were angry at me because of what I was doing, but that just made me do it all the more. The more they wanted me to stop, the less I got the support I needed to stop. One big ugly circle.

BENNY

When my wife walked out on me and took our teenage son, I knew *it was the end. I just wasn't sure right away if it was the end of my family or the end of my drinking. I chose my marriage and son over alcohol. My family saved my life, and I had a lot to make up for.*

PEOPLE WITH ADDICTIONS seek help or treatment for many reasons. Sometimes they boldly decide for themselves that the time has come to regain their life, but often external factors such as health issues, legal trouble, or work-related disciplinary actions push the addict into some kind of treatment. Because addictions erode and frequently destroy relationships, pressure to get help often comes from a spouse or partner.

Under the best of circumstances relationships can be difficult to build and sustain, but for the addict or person involved with the addict, staying in a healthy relationship is an uphill battle. Some relationships that *can* sustain an addiction are "codependent"; that is, both parties share addictive or other behaviors that are counterproductive to individual growth. Sometimes relationships are tenuously held together because of the needs of the children or financial reliance.

Some relationships that can sustain an addiction are "codependent": that is, both parties share addictive or other behaviors that are counterproductive to individual growth.

The primary goal of the addict is to sustain and feed the addiction. As the addiction progresses, everything else, including relationships, becomes secondary. Addicts have been known to deceive, steal from, neglect, and abuse the needs of spouses, romantic partners, children, and friends.

If you've worked through the tasks of earlier chapters, you should be at a point in your recovery where you're willing to make significant changes and repair damage to your relationships. Addicts who are not yet committed to their *own* recovery are unlikely to be able to make serious commitments to other people.

Lopsided Relationships

Relationships are a two-way street, affecting the individuals on both ends of the relationship. In families, there are multiple relationships going on at the same time: between spouses, between parents and children, and between siblings. In extended families, the interactions become more complicated still, including grandparents, uncles, aunts, and cousins.

Reduced to their essence, however, all relationships are between just two people: you and the other person. It is at this level that relationships ultimately succeed or fail. Although both parties contribute to the success or failure of the relationship, in relationships where one person (or both) is an addict, the relationship is lopsided and unstable. The normal patterns of the relationship are placed under special pressure. Addicts in relationships often require a special focus on *their* needs without being able (or willing) to provide an equal focus on the needs of the other person. Relationships are often bent around the needs of the addict. Consequently, addictions take a tremendous toll on the other people in the relationship, whose needs and desires go unmet, whose energies are expended on managing the addiction and trying to keep it in check, and whose own best interests are not acted on.

In any developed addiction (where an addiction has clearly begun to significantly affect the life of the addict), chances are the addiction has also affected the addict's relationships in some way.

Damaged Relationships

In any developed addiction (where an addiction has clearly begun to significantly affect the life of the addict), chances are the addiction has also affected the addict's relationships in some way. Perhaps a supervisor has begun to notice excessive tardiness, or maybe a former spouse is suing for sole custody of the children. Damage can vary widely and become more serious if left unchecked.

Use the next journal entry to take stock of the state of your relationships.

THINKING ABOUT YOUR RELATIONSHIPS

1. Generally describe your relationships.

_____

_____

_____

_____

2. Are your relationships important to you?

_____

_____

_____

_____

3. What are the most satisfying aspects of your relationships?

_____

_____

_____

_____

4. What are the least satisfying aspects?

_____

_____

_____

_____

5. How are you the most supported and strengthened by your relationships?

_____

_____

_____

_____

6. How are you the most hurt and let down by your relationships?

_____

_____

_____

_____

7. How do you most support and strengthen the people with whom you have important relationships?

_____

_____

_____

_____

8. How do you most hurt or let down these people?

_____

_____

_____

_____

9. How has your addiction affected your most important relationships?

_____

_____

_____

_____

_____

THINGS TO THINK ABOUT

- If addiction has affected your relationships, what sort of effect will recovery have on them?
- Do you need to make repairs to your relationships? What sort of repairs are needed?

Changing Relationships

Relationships are dynamic; they rarely stay the same over time. Some become closer, more intimate, and stronger. Others become more distant. People change and drift apart. Sometimes it's the demanding nature of addiction that wedges a relationship apart.

Relationships are dynamic; they rarely stay the same over time.

How have your relationships changed and, more to the point, why? Have your relationships simply evolved and shifted over time, or has your addiction wedged itself between you and other people? Perhaps your addiction has strengthened your relationships. This would be unusual, but there have been instances in which a family member or friend has pitched in to help and in the process the relationship grew. However, even under such circumstances if the addiction isn't resolved over time, it will eventually wedge people apart. If addiction has resulted in bonding and made your relationships closer, ask yourself if these are codependent relationships.

The next journal entry will help you focus on how your relationships have changed over time.

CHANGING TIMES

1. List five of your most important relationships. Next to each briefly describe why each is important.

Relationship	Importance
a. _____	_____
b. _____	_____
c. _____	_____
d. _____	_____
e. _____	_____

2. Have any of these relationships changed over time? If so, which ones have changed, and why? _____

_____

_____

_____

3. How has your addiction affected these important relationships?

_____

_____

_____

_____

4. What can you do to improve these relationships?

_____

_____

_____

_____

THINGS TO THINK ABOUT

- Has your addiction brought about changes in your relationships? What sort of changes might recovery bring about?
- If your addiction has strengthened any of your relationships or brought you closer to people, is this a healthy trend? Are your relationships codependent?

One Relationship at a Time

Use the next entry to focus on how your relationships have been negatively affected by your addiction and which of those relationships have been affected the most. This entry focuses on a single relationship, so use it repeatedly to write about each relationship that has been negatively affected.

REPAIRING RELATIONSHIPS

1. Which of your relationships have most clearly and definitely been affected by your addiction?

_____   _____

_____   _____

_____   _____

_____   _____

_____   _____

_____   _____

2. *My addiction has most affected these relationships by* . . . _____

_____

_____

_____

_____

3. Choose one of the relationships from Question 1, and describe the way your addiction has affected it. Relationship: _____

a. *The impact of my addiction on this relationship has been* . . . _____

_____

_____

b. *I've allowed this to happen because* . . . _____

_____

_____

c. *When I think about the damage caused to this relationship, I* . . . _____

_____

_____

d. *What I want most from this relationship is . . .* _____

_____

_____

e. *I can repair damage to this relationship by . . .* _____

_____

_____

f. *I can most strengthen this relationship by . . .* _____

_____

_____

Scapegoating and Displaced Feelings

In blaming others, people often fail to recognize where blame *ought* to lie. When we blame others for things *we* are responsible for, we're both failing to take personal responsibility and wrongly making a scapegoat out of someone else. Not only is it unfair to that person, it frankly doesn't work. The blame and responsibility still remain with us, despite our refusing to acknowledge them.

Sometimes when people fail to recognize the source of their negative feelings (or fail to recognize that they even *have* feelings), they inappropriately displace them onto someone or something else. They may be upset with someone at work, for instance, but

People with active addictions often blame others and displace their feelings. They want or need to assign blame to someone else (scapegoating), or they fail to recognize that their behaviors are a reaction to something else (displacement).

take it out on the kids when they get home. Displacement usually happens without your being conscious of it. Trying to quell a feeling or not noticing that you're having one doesn't make it go away. Instead, it gets expressed—usually inappropriately—through displacement. You may believe you're reacting to the right person, but you're really fooling yourself into believing that the responsibility lies with someone other than yourself.

People with active addictions often blame others and displace their feelings. They want or need to assign blame to someone else (scapegoating), or they fail to recognize that their behaviors are a reaction to something else (displacement). Neither behavior is good for relationship building.

Use the next entry to think about whether you scapegoat or displace your feelings onto other people.

SCAPEGOATS

1. Do you blame others for your behaviors or problems? If so, who do you blame and why?

_____

_____

_____

_____

2. Describe an instance when you recently held someone else to blame for a problem, something that happened, or some feeling you had.

_____

_____

_____

_____

_____

3. Think about *your* responsibility for what happened or how you felt. Describe the situation from a different perspective, in which you hold responsibility for what happened or how you felt.

_____

_____

_____

_____

_____

4. Do you ever displace your feelings? If so, onto who or what?

_____

_____

_____

_____

_____

5. Describe a recent situation in which you displaced your feelings about one situation onto another person.

_____

_____

_____

_____

_____

6. Do scapegoating and displacement affect your relationships? If so, how?

_____

_____

_____

_____

_____

Destructive Relationships

It would be a mistake to assume that every relationship problem is the addict's fault. Many problems are caused mutually by both people in the relationship, and some are caused solely by the nonaddicted party.

It would be a mistake to assume that every relationship problem is the addict's fault. Many problems are caused mutually by both people in the relationship, some are caused solely by the non-addicted party. Sometimes the very root of the addiction can be traced to a past (or current) relationship made destructive by an abusing spouse or neglectful parent. Regardless of the addiction's cause, it is up to the addict to recognize these issues and accept responsibility for the addiction itself. However, exploring relationships from the past can provide insight into current relationships.

Use the next entry to think about past relationships that were destructive to you in some way. Repeat the entry if you want to write about more than one past relationship.

THROUGH THE PAST DARKLY

1. Describe a past relationship that had an undermining effect on your sense of self-esteem because of the behavior of the other person or people in the relationship.

_____

_____

_____

_____

_____

_____

2. In what way was this relationship destructive or damaging to you?

_____

_____

_____

_____

_____

3. How did that past relationship affect or shape your self-esteem?

_____

_____

_____

_____

4. How did that past relationship affect or contribute to your addiction?

_____

_____

_____

_____

5. How does this past relationship affect you today?

_____

_____

_____

_____

6. What can you learn about your *present* relationships by thinking back on past relationships that were destructive to you?

_____

_____

_____

_____

Current Destructive Relationships

What present relationships are destructive to you, contribute to poor self-image, or otherwise fail to meet your needs? Can you do anything about them?

The purpose of the next entry is *not* to provide you with a rationale for addiction but instead to help you bring honest insight to your relationships in terms of how they might be hurting you (and how you might be hurting them). Use this entry repeatedly to evaluate any or all of your current relationships in which you are in some way victimized.

DAMAGE CONTROL

1. List a current relationship in which there is some *active* element that undermines or damages you.

_____

_____

_____

_____

_____

2. Check off any words that describe the ways in which this relationship is harmful to you, and add others below.

__abusive, mentally   __demoralizing   __intimidating

__abusive, physically   __dishonest   __manipulative

__coercive   __dismissive   __neglectful

__controlling   __dominating   __oppressive

__demanding   __hostile   __repressive

__demeaning   __insulting   __threatening

other:_____   _____

_____   _____

_____   _____

3. Describe how this relationship is destructive or harmful to you.

_____

_____

_____

_____

4. Is the damage intentional? Does the other person *mean* to harm you?

_____

_____

_____

_____

5. Is the damage direct? Is it caused by what the other person is actually doing or what the other person is *failing* to do?

_____

_____

_____

_____

6. Is the damage conscious or unconscious? Does the other person *know* that he or she is causing damage?

_____

_____

_____

_____

_____

7. Is the damage imposed on you in this relationship a reaction to your addiction, or is your addiction fueled by the damage? Which came first?

_____

_____

_____

_____

_____

8. What can you do to stop the destructive quality of this relationship?

_____

_____

_____

_____

_____

THINGS TO THINK ABOUT

- How long have you been aware that this relationship was destructive to you? Why have you let the destruction persist?
- Can this relationship be repaired? If so, are you willing to work toward repair? If not, are you willing to end it?
- Are you also destructive in this relationship?

Relationships Are Important

Relationships are important. They're our connection to others, and without them we're cut off from the world. Relationships give us information about ourselves and how we're seen and valued by others. The health of our relationships is measured by the respect and support we put into them and also by that which we're able to take from them.

The health of our relationships is measured by the respect and support we put into them and also by that which we're able to take from them.

Use the final journal entry in this chapter to assess what you've learned about the relationships in your life.

CHECKPOINT: RELATIONSHIPS

1. What have you learned about your relationships?

_____

_____

_____

2. What have you learned about your relationship needs?

_____

_____

_____

3. What have you learned about how to deal with your relationships?

_____

_____

_____

4. Do you feel a need to make any substantial changes in your relationships?

_____

_____

_____

"Sickness is felt, but
health not at all."
—THOMAS FULLER

14

Destination:
GOOD HEALTH—REBUILDING
BODY, MIND, AND SPIRIT

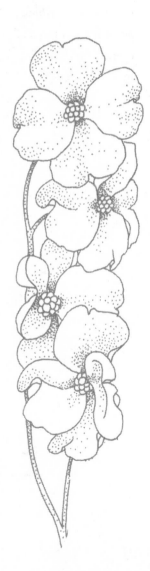

CARRIE

I was ill, and I mean ill in the greatest sense of the word. I never took care of my health, and every time I got stressed it became an excuse to do all the things that either made me unhealthy or kept me unhealthy. When I look back at photos of myself from then, you can actually see just how rough I looked. The sad thing is that I didn't know it at the time. My mental health was—well, I didn't have any *mental health; I mean, I wasn't mentally ill, but I sure didn't have mental hygiene. But maybe worst of all, I was empty inside. I couldn't find fulfillment or meaning anywhere in my life. I felt like a burned-out shell. That illness kept making me even more ill. It was an illness of spirit that invaded my soul, mind, and body.*

YOU NO DOUBT notice the ill health brought to you and your life by your addiction, or someone else has. Possibly that's the reason you picked this book up in the first place. The goal of this chapter is for you to experience, perhaps for the first time, physical, emotional, and spiritual health.

Body, Mind, and Spirit

"Wellness" involves more than just physical health. As defined by the World Health Organization, health is not simply the absence of illness but a state of *physical, mental,* and *social* well-being. Begin thinking about your recovery in terms of your physical, emotional, and spiritual health and how to balance these three aspects.

Health is not simply the absence of illness but a state of physical, mental, and social well-being.

A healthy body requires no explanation. Emotional or mental health refers to a state of mind that is comfortable or comforting, such as clarity of thought, peacefulness and serenity, or confidence. But what is meant by spiritual health?

Spirituality refers to the sense of meaning you *derive* from your life and your world as well as the meaning you *infuse* into the world. The word *spirit* then may be thought of as the animating or the motivating force that drives us. For some people, spiritual life is more connected to their *sense* of well-being than is body or mind.

Well-being means healthy body, healthy mind, and healthy spiritual self; without one, the others are compromised. Anxiety, depression, and other mental health issues often contribute to problems with physical health. Similarly those who find little meaning in the world discover that their spiritual malaise has a detrimental influence on both their mental and physical well-being.

Wellness

Based on the work of the John D. and Catherine T. MacArthur Foundation midlife development project, wellness can be defined by six characteristics.

1. *Self-acceptance* is a sense of personal satisfaction and a healthy self-image, regardless of the direction one's life has taken.

2. *Purpose* is a set of values and goals that give direction and lend meaning to life.

3. *Environmental mastery* is the ability to manage the tasks and demands of everyday life.

4. *Personal growth* is a sense of accomplishment, personal competency, and continued development.

5. *Positive relationships* are successful ones that provide meaningful ties to the larger world.

6. *Autonomy* is a sense of independence and self-determination.

Use the next journal entry to think about your sense of wellness and well-being.

EMOTIONAL AND SPIRITUAL WELLNESS

1. Describe your sense of self-satisfaction.

_____

_____

_____

_____

2. On this 1 to 5 scale, circle the number that most approximates how you view your self-image.

Negative Self-Image:			Positive Self-Image:	
I see myself as really ineffective.			*I see myself as really effective.*	
1	2	3	4	5

3. Explain your answer. How do you see yourself, and why?

_____

_____

_____

4. On this 1 to 5 scale, circle the number that most approximates your level of satisfaction with your life right now.

Dissatisfied	Satisfied
I'm very dissatisfied with my life.	*I'm very satisfied with my life.*

1   2   3   4   5

5. How do you feel about your accomplishments in life?

_____

_____

_____

_____

6. Do you feel a sense of mastery and competency in your daily life?

_____

_____

_____

_____

7. Does your life have meaning at this time, a sense of purpose or direction?

_____

_____

_____

_____

8. Do you feel in control of your life and where it's going?

_____

_____

_____

_____

9. Are you satisfied with your current relationships? Do they provide meaningful ties to the world around you?

_____

_____

_____

_____

THINGS TO THINK ABOUT

- Did you find any of your answers difficult to accept? If so, why?
- What does this inventory tell you about yourself, your needs, and your desires at this time in your life? Should you return to this entry again in a few weeks?

Emotional Health

Whereas you can eat better, exercise more, and do other tangible things that clearly affect your physical well-being, it's a little more difficult to define the things that improve or help maintain mental or emotional health. They are intangible—things you can discuss but can't see or touch—but their impact is concrete. Learning to relax, for example, a mental activity that is aimed more at your psyche than your physical body, results in both improved mental and physical health. Likewise, positive, supportive relationships bolster mental health and foster a sense of personal connectedness at the same time, thus improving spiritual health also.

Positive, supportive relationships bolster mental health and foster a sense of personal connectedness at the same time, thus improving spiritual health also.

Spiritual Health

In many self-help programs that are based on the AA model, there is an emphasis on the spiritual side of recovery. Often the term *higher power* is used to describe this sense of spirituality and connectedness to something outside of yourself, but spirituality in this sense has nothing to do with religion or a belief in a god per se. Instead, the crux of spirituality is finding meaning in life, thereby developing or renewing a sense of attachment, purpose, and the inner calm that often comes with spiritual health. Many addicts have lost hope or cannot find meaning anywhere.

Health and Relaxation

The ability to relax is an important tool for maintaining mental, spiritual, and physical health. Not being able to do so carries a big price tag: physical and emotional fatigue, tension and stress, worry and anxiety, and a constant state of being on the edge. Allowing addiction to help you relax or manage stress is unproductive and ineffective. Addictions simply increase stress, providing anything but relief and relaxation, and they make no meaningful contributions to your well-being.

However, there are many positive and effective ways to relax, though you may need to learn them. You might unwind by drinking a cup of tea or cocoa or by watching television. Some people learn self-hypnosis techniques or learn to "visualize" themselves in a favorite spot and relaxed mood. Others meditate or practice yoga, employ techniques for muscle and breath relaxation, or simply exercise.

The next journal entry will help you evaluate the relationship between relaxation and physical health in your life.

PHYSICAL HEALTH AND RELAXATION

1. Is taking care of yourself physically a problem?

_____

_____

_____

_____

2. Which areas of your physical health concern you the most? Have these become concerns only recently, or have they always been so?

_____

_____

_____

_____

_____

3. What most prevents you from being able to relax?

_____

_____

_____

_____

4. What are the greatest areas of stress in your life right now?

_____

_____

_____

_____

5. Check off all methods of relaxation you currently use and those you might find helpful to try. Add others below, including ineffective, potentially harmful relaxation techniques (for example, medicating yourself with alcohol or drugs, gambling, engaging in unhealthy eating or sexual activities).

__breathing control   __meditation   __self-hypnosis   __walking

__cup of tea   __quiet music   __sports   __warm bath

__exercise   __reading   __talking   __writing

__making art   __relaxation tapes   __television/radio   __yoga

6. Do any of your preferred ways to relax include your addiction or anything equally unhealthy?

_____

_____

_____

7. What can you do to learn to relax more completely?

_____

_____

_____

8. How do you see the relationship among physical, mental, and spiritual health?

_____

_____

_____

_____

THINGS TO THINK ABOUT

- Is relaxing a problem for you? What most interferes with your ability to relax? How can you overcome these obstacles?
- Do others ever express a concern that you don't relax enough or that you relax in ways that are unhealthy?
- What do you need to do or change to take better care of your emotional, spiritual, and physical health?

Breathing for Health

Breathing and relaxation exercises can change both physical and mental states by affecting brain wave patterns, relaxing muscles, and even influencing the capacity to learn. Deep breathing exercises the lungs to maximum capacity and fully oxygenates the blood. Deep breathing and breath control exercises are recommended by dozens of health books, health training programs, and spiritual disciplines as a key to relaxation, meditation, and wellness. Take some time now to breathe deeply and completely, and then complete the next journal entry in this chapter.

Take five deep breaths, clear your mind, and physically and mentally relax for about five minutes. The relaxation is as important as the deep breathing it follows. Complete the entry in this relaxed state of mind.

Breathing and relaxation exercises can change both physical and mental states by affecting brain wave patterns, relaxing muscles, and even influencing the capacity to learn.

A BREATH OF LIFE

1. Describe the experience of deep breathing and relaxation by completing these sentences.

a. *Breathing this way makes me feel . . .* _____

_____

_____

b. *With each breath, I . . .* _____

_____

c. *Breathing this way opens me up to . . .* _____

_____

_____

d. *Breathing this way symbolizes my journey by . . .* _____

_____

_____

2. What thoughts or feelings ran through your mind *as you breathed?*

_____

_____

_____

3. What thoughts or feelings ran through your mind *as you relaxed after the breathing exercise?*

_____

_____

_____

THINGS TO THINK ABOUT

- Do you usually stop to breathe deeply during your day? If not, what was it like to concentrate in this way, shutting out the things that perhaps normally distract you from your own body?
- Is this an entry worth repeating, perhaps even daily?
- What can deep breathing teach you about personal health care?

Contemplation and Daily Affirmations

The relaxation and breathing exercises you just completed help you maintain good health by separating your mind and body from emotional stress. Contemplation is also tied to the ability to relax. One tool that many people use for contemplation is daily affirmations.

Daily affirmations are usually based on a thought for that day, often inspirational or offering some form of guidance. They can provide a focal point for the entire day to which you can repeatedly return during the course of the day. Daily affirmations can be:

- *energizing*, helping you find the strength to work through difficult days

- *inspirational*, offering guidance and wisdom to help deal with daily issues

- *self-affirming*, reconfirming and strengthening your belief in yourself

- *soothing*, providing calming and comforting thoughts to focus on throughout the day

Morning affirmations set the pace for the day and provide an anchor to help you get through difficult times. Evening affirmations are a way to reflect on and resolve the issues of the day. Between them, they're a powerful tool for finding and building emotional peace in your daily life.

The next journal entry runs over seven days. First, collect seven inspirational verses that will serve as daily affirmation for each of the seven days. The words you choose may come from any number of sources, including quotations, song lyrics, poetry, scriptures, or other inspirational works. Then follow these steps.

Morning affirmations set the pace for the day and provide an anchor to help you get through difficult times. Evening affirmations are a way to reflect on and resolve the issues of the day.

- Each morning record your affirmation for that day on your journal entry. Write a few words that reflect on its meaning to you, and the reason you chose these words as your affirmation for the day.

- As you move through your day, think about how your day is going and how you're feeling. Each time you contemplate your day, recall your daily affirmation. Think about its meaning and why you chose it for that day.

- At the end of your day, contemplate the affirmation you chose.

- Complete the entry after seven days of daily affirmations.

DAILY AFFIRMATIONS

1. Write your daily affirmation for each of the seven days, one day at a time.

DAY 1

My daily affirmation: _____

_____

_____

I chose these words because . . . _____

_____

DAY 2

My daily affirmation: _____

_____

_____

I chose these words because . . . _____

_____

DAY 3

My daily affirmation: _____

_____

_____

I chose these words because . . . _____

_____

DAY 4

My daily affirmation: _____

_____

_____

I chose these words because . . . _____

_____

DAY 5

My daily affirmation: _____

_____

_____

I chose these words because . . . _____

_____

DAY 6

My daily affirmation: _____

_____

_____

I chose these words because . . . _____

_____

DAY 7

My daily affirmation: _____

_____

_____

I chose these words because . . . _____

_____

2. Did using daily affirmations help the contemplative process throughout and at the end of each day?

_____

_____

_____

3. What did you most learn about yourself?

_____

_____

_____

Health and Humor

The ability to laugh at our own weaknesses and flaws gives us a tool to manage our most difficult feelings and overcome obstacles we may face.

Humor is no laughing matter. The ability to laugh at our own weaknesses and flaws gives us a tool to manage our most difficult feelings and overcome obstacles we may face. Health and humor are integrally connected; the healing power of humor has been well documented by many authors, including Paul McGhee, Normal Cousins, William Fry, and Joel Goodman.

Each day for the next two weeks, find something that makes you laugh. It can be a newspaper or magazine cartoon, a TV show, a funny movie, or a book—anything that makes you chuckle. Complete this journal entry at the end of the two weeks.

MAKE 'EM LAUGH

1. How did humor affect your day?

_____

_____

_____

2. Was there a theme to the things that made you laugh?

_____

_____

_____

3. What can you learn about yourself from the things that made you laugh?

_____

_____

_____

_____

4. How does humor add to your life?

_____

_____

_____

_____

THINGS TO THINK ABOUT

- Can you laugh at yourself? Do you allow others to laugh at you?
- Is it possible to find humor in *any* situation? If so, how can you apply this thinking to your addiction? If not, why not?
- Is it important to keep *finding* things to laugh at every day?

Take a Hike

One of the easiest methods for exercising body, mind, and soul all at the same time requires no special equipment, sophisticated techniques, or membership fees. Walking is something you do just by stepping outdoors. Walking every day can tone up your muscles, help you lose weight, get your heart pumping, and improve your overall health. Your pace and destination are up to you. Consider taking a walk several times each week, if not every day. Walk your dog, stroll with your partner or your children, take a lunch break and hike to a lake, or get out among the crowds on the city streets.

One of the easiest methods for exercising body, mind, and soul all at the same time requires no special equipment, sophisticated techniques, or membership fees. Walking is something you do just by stepping outdoors.

The next journal entry should be completed *after* you've taken a walk. Any kind of walk will do; just make sure you take your mind along as well. This walk will exercise your senses as well as your body. It is designed to get you in touch with your health, your sense of wellness, and the world around you. By opening your mind and using your senses to let things in, you exercise your spirit as well. Read the journal entry before you leave for your walk, and familiarize yourself with the questions it poses. Be sure to bring a notebook with you. While on your walk, periodically stop, think about the questions asked, and jot down your thoughts, experiences, and ideas in your notebook. Complete the journal entry immediately upon returning from your walk, so your ideas and energy will still be fresh.

EXERCISING YOUR BODY, MIND, AND SOUL

1. What kind of walk did you take today?

_____

_____

2. Complete these sentences to describe your walk.

I walked along . . . _____

_____

I walked through . . . _____

_____

Along the way, I . . . _____

_____

3. What did you notice that you'd never noticed before?

_____

_____

_____

4. What smells did you most notice?

_____

_____

_____

_____

5. What colors stood out the most for you, and why?

_____

_____

_____

_____

6. What sounds could you pick out, near and far?

_____

_____

_____

_____

7. What interesting textures did you stop and feel?

_____

_____

_____

_____

8. What did you see of special interest?

_____

_____

_____

9. What did you think about on your walk?

_____

_____

_____

Community and Service to Others

Considerable data suggest that involvement in a community cuts down on vulnerability to infection, decreases heart disease, and has positive effects on both mental and physical health. However, getting connected with your community is not something that can be done in a week. It's a lifelong project.

There's more to being connected to a community than just the sense of belonging you derive from it. . . . Community service allows you to give back to others the support you received when it was most needed.

There's more to being connected to a community than just the sense of belonging *you* derive from it. In fact, it shouldn't be a self-serving act at all. Community service allows you to give back to others the support you received when it was most needed. Giving to your community is a way of expressing your gratitude for being able to live and enjoy your life. It nourishes your own spiritual health while nurturing others too.

How you choose to serve your community is up to you. You can do so anonymously by cleaning up litter in a local park, or you can choose a more visible role by working in a soup kitchen, coaching a local children's team, mowing an elderly neighbor's lawn, or volunteering at a nearby hospital or library. Remember to pace yourself so that you don't burn out by overextending yourself. Most important, don't commit yourself at all unless you have the time, skills, energy, and discipline to follow through on your commitment.

For the next two weeks do something each day to help someone, make your community a better place to live in, or make your workplace a better place to work. Concentrate on *small* acts of service initially; you can always increase your level of commitment later. For each of the fourteen days, use the following journal entry to note what you did and how it made you feel. At the end of the two weeks, complete the entry. Start your entry by thinking about some of the things you can do for others.

SERVICE TO OTHERS

1. Make a list of a dozen services you can perform for your community, a specific group or organization, or a particular person.

a. _____   g. _____

b. _____   h. _____

c. _____   i. _____

d. _____   j. _____

e. _____   k. _____

f. _____   l. _____

2. At the end of each day, describe briefly what you did that day and how it made you feel. Continue on to Question 3 only when you've finished your full fourteen-day service.

	What You Did	*How It Made You Feel*
Day 1:	_____	_____
Day 2:	_____	_____
Day 3:	_____	_____
Day 4:	_____	_____
Day 5:	_____	_____
Day 6:	_____	_____
Day 7:	_____	_____
Day 8:	_____	_____

	What You Did	*How It Made You Feel*
Day 9:	_____	_____
Day 10:	_____	_____
Day 11:	_____	_____
Day 12:	_____	_____
Day 13:	_____	_____
Day 14:	_____	_____

3. How did it feel to complete community service?

_____

_____

_____

_____

4. What was the most difficult part of providing service?

_____

_____

_____

_____

5. What was the most gratifying aspect of providing service?

_____

_____

_____

_____

6. What did you most learn about yourself from this experience?

_____

_____

_____

7. What did you most learn about others?

_____

_____

_____

_____

8. What did you most learn about body, mind, and spiritual health?

_____

_____

_____

_____

THINGS TO THINK ABOUT

- Was any part of community service humbling, humiliating, or embarrassing? If so, why was it and how did you deal with? Are you a humble person by nature?
- Is service to others important to your spiritual health? Is it something that you want to continue giving?

15

Destination:

UNFINISHED BUSINESS

CHRIS

I hated this part of my recovery. Everything else seemed easy compared with having to look at all those things left undone in my life and, worse, all those things I'd done to other people to keep my addiction going. I'd lied to the people I loved and who trusted me the most and stolen from them in every way. I'd cheated everyone and wasn't there for my own kids when they most needed me. I don't think I really knew it at the time (or maybe I did but just didn't care), but as I became straight and sober it became very clear to me. It was so hard to look at myself in that way, and even harder to actually have to do something about it and ask for forgiveness. Maybe the things that are the hardest are also the most cleansing because once I'd accomplished that work I felt freer than I had in years.

JON

There were so many things holding me back. Things I'd done, things people had done to me, and things that were left undone. I was full of guilt, anger, and remorse, all bundled together. It wasn't until I tackled those leftover things and straightened up my affairs that I was able to really get on with my life.

THE FINAL STAGE of your recovery has no end; your work in this stage will continue through your entire life. Like life in general, no matter how far you've come there's still further to go. This chapter wraps up some of your Stage 4 work by looking at unresolved issues from past and present relationships and finding ways to come to terms with them, as well as transitioning into the active recovery of Stage 5. For many addicts, this will also entail making amends for past actions.

Unfinished Business

The things you never did and the things you could have done differently. The words you should have said or those you wish you hadn't spoken. The unresolved issues, differences, and feelings. The unfulfilled plans and expectations. This is the stuff of unfinished business. In a world of chaos, people seek order; in a life of loose ends, they seek closure.

Achieving closure isn't always possible. . . . Sometimes you must learn to accept that unfinished business is going to remain unfinished.

Seeking Closure

Although you undoubtedly have strong feelings about your relationships and experiences, unfinished business is not about those *feelings*. It is about the unresolved situations and relationships themselves.

Sometimes issues from former relationships can be resolved simply by talking to the person with whom you have unfinished business. You may find, however, that achieving closure isn't always possible. Perhaps your ex-spouse has no desire to hear your regrets about the irreparable damage your addiction caused to the marriage, or maybe a loved one's death is preventing you from voicing all that you need to say. Sometimes you must learn to accept that unfinished business is going to remain unfinished.

Although you may not be ready to raise or resolve your unfinished business with others right now, your journal is an excellent place to examine these issues with yourself. Use the next journal entry to voice your thoughts on all aspects of your life in which you seek closure. Use this entry repeatedly, each time using it to think about and express issues that are important or left unsettled for you.

EXPRESSING YOUR FEELINGS

"Grant me the serenity to accept the things I cannot change,
the courage to change the things I can,
and the wisdom to know the difference."
—REINHOLD NIEBUHR

1. Describe a relationship, situation, or interaction that was left hanging or unresolved for you.

_____

_____

_____

_____

2. Complete the sentence for each feeling that applies for you. Add others below.

I feel angry because . . . _____

I feel apologetic because . . . _____

I feel ashamed because . . . _____

I feel betrayed because . . . _____

I feel cheated because . . . _____

I feel crushed because . . . _____

I feel curious because . . . _____

I feel doubtful because . . . _____

I feel exploited because . . . _____

I feel guilty because . . . _____

I feel hurt because . . . _____

I feel irritated because . . . _____

I feel mistreated because . . . _____

I feel offended because . . . _____

I feel regretful because . . . _____

I feel resentful because . . . _____

I feel vengeful because . . . _____

I feel _____ *because . . .* _____

I feel _____ *because . . .* _____

I feel _____ *because . . .* _____

3. Which of these feelings or issues is most pressing for you right now? Why?

_____

_____

_____

_____

4. What makes this unfinished business for you?

_____

_____

_____

_____

5. What about this issue is left undone?

_____

_____

_____

_____

6. What do you want to say to the other person or people involved in this piece of unfinished business?

_____

_____

_____

_____

THINGS TO THINK ABOUT

- Does thinking and writing about this issue help you better understand this piece of unfinished business?
- Does writing about this piece of unfinished business help get it off your mind? Do you need to revisit this piece of unfinished business again to work on resolving your feelings about it?
- If the other person or people involved in your unfinished business are still available to you, should you seek closure or let it go? Think carefully about your decision and its possible consequences.

Expressing Regret

Addressing unfinished business sometimes requires little more than voicing regret for things done (or left undone). Expressing regret isn't a matter of wishing away that which has passed. Instead, it's a way to express sorrow and remorse for a missed opportunity, a way to exorcise and relieve yourself of an otherwise unspoken burden. Expressing regret does not change what happened in the past, but it can transform the present.

Expressing regret does not change what happened in the past, but it can transform the present.

Use the next journal entry to revisit a missed opportunity and discover how the power of words—*your* words—can transform shapeless feelings into meaningful ideas. Again, this is an entry to use repeatedly.

MISSED OPPORTUNITY

1. Describe a relationship, situation, or interaction that in some way represents a missed opportunity for you.

_____

_____

_____

_____

2. Complete these sentences, which describe your regrets.

a. *I wish I'd said . . .* _____

_____

b. *I wish you'd said . . .* _____

_____

c. *I wish I had . . .* _____

_____

d. *I wish I hadn't . . .* _____

_____

e. *I wish you had . . .* _____

_____

f. *I wish you hadn't . . .* _____

_____

g. *I wish I could change . . .* _____

_____

h. *I'm sorry for . . .* _____

_____

i. *I wish . . .* _____

_____

3. Describe how you might resolve this regret, restore this missed opportunity, or close this unfinished business.

_____

_____

_____

_____

THINGS TO THINK ABOUT

- Some people wish their lives away, pondering over past regrets or things left undone. Will you use this entry to wish things were different or to take action?
- What sort of role did your addiction play in creating this piece of unfinished business?

Direct and Indirect Restitution

Resolving unfinished business relieves you of the "excess baggage" that can weigh down your physical, mental, and spiritual well-being and interfere with your relationships with others. Unburdening yourself is important, but resolving unfinished business involves more than just healing yourself. Sometimes repayment is required, not through discussion, debate, or explanation but through restitution.

Think about past relationships for which you seek closure. Was the damage to these relationships that resulted from your addiction conscious and direct, or was harm inflicted indirectly or unintentionally? Did you steal people's money, reputation, or trust? Did you take advantage of them? Did your addiction make unreasonable demands on their time? These are examples of conscious, direct harm. Were you neglectful? Did your child miss out on important events because you were busy meeting your ad-

Resolving unfinished business involves more than just healing yourself. Sometimes repayment is required, not through discussion, debate, or explanation but through restitution.

diction's needs? These are examples of indirect or unintentional harm.

To effect long-term recovery, you must actively work toward restoring and repairing these relationships, even if the people to whom restitution is due are no longer available. For instance, if you once stole a car and have no way of knowing whose car it was, you can donate an equivalent sum of time or money to a charity. If it's impossible to apologize or make amends to someone in your past who is no longer in your life now, you can pay restitution by apologizing or paying more attention to someone in your present life. There are many ways to make indirect amends, but the more direct and open the restitution, the more direct and open the healing.

Use the next journal entry to create a list of *everyone* with whom you must make amends and to begin thinking about making restitution.

DOING THE RIGHT THING

1. Make a list of people you have harmed in some way. If your list is long, continue it on a separate sheet of paper. Make the list as complete as possible.

Person	*Harm Caused*
_____	_____
_____	_____
_____	_____
_____	_____
_____	_____
_____	_____
_____	_____

2. For every person you listed in Question 1, think of at least one way in which you might make direct amends to them. If making direct amends is not possible, or might cause further harm to them, list a way to make indirect amends.

Person	Restitution/Amends
_____	_____
_____	_____
_____	_____
_____	_____
_____	_____
_____	_____
_____	_____
_____	_____

3. What was it like to create this list?

_____

_____

_____

_____

4. How does the idea of making amends make you feel?

_____

_____

_____

5. What will be the most difficult aspect of making restitution?

_____

_____

_____

_____

6. Are you ready to make amends?

_____

_____

_____

_____

7. What must you overcome in yourself to make amends?

_____

_____

_____

_____

THINGS TO THINK ABOUT

- Does making amends require humility? Are you a humble person?
- Are there some people to whom it will be especially difficult to make amends? If so, why? What is it about these people—or you—that will make it difficult?
- Do you believe it's important to make amends and pay restitution for harm you've caused to others?

Getting Personal

Building on the previous entry, use the next journal entry to focus your thoughts on one individual to whom you should make amends. Repeat the entry for everyone on the list you created on page 268. Remember, the primary goal is to make amends to the *other* person, not make yourself feel better.

MAKING AMENDS

1. Choose one person from your list, and focus the rest of this entry on that person.

_____

2. How have you harmed this person?

_____

_____

_____

_____

3. Was the harm intentional and direct or unintentional and indirect?

_____

_____

_____

_____

4. Whether intentional or unintentional, were you conscious and aware of the harm at the time you caused it, or did you become aware of the harm only later? If later, when did you first become aware of the harm caused?

_____

_____

_____

_____

5. Did the harm occur on a single occasion, or did it take place over an extended period of time?

_____

_____

_____

_____

6. How can you best make amends to this person?

_____

_____

_____

_____

7. What will prevent you from making amends?

_____

_____

_____

_____

8. What will it be like to make amends?

_____

_____

_____

_____

Complete the next question only *after* you have begun to make amends.
9. What was it like to make amends?

_____

_____

_____

_____

_____

_____

_____

_____

Letting Go

Sometimes you must accept that some unfinished business just can't be resolved. In such cases you need to learn to let go. Letting go is difficult, but *not* letting go is even harder because emotional wounds that don't heal will stay with you for the rest of your life.

People have different methods for letting go. Some are able to simply push old baggage out of their minds and move on, but if you require a more "active" approach, try writing a letter, expressing your regrets and how you'd make amends if you could. Even if you don't send it, just the act of writing can be cathartic. Getting rid of a photograph or other mementos that keep old feelings alive can also help. Throw yourself a party to commemorate your freedom from the oppression of unresolvable business. Letting go is liberating.

Use your experiences with unfinished business from your past to ensure that today's relationships and issues don't become *tomorrow's* unfinished business.

Letting go is difficult, but not letting go is even harder because emotional wounds that don't heal will stay with you for the rest of your life.

LETTING GO

1. What have you learned about unfinished business?

_____

_____

_____

_____

2. What have you learned about resolving unfinished business?

_____

_____

_____

3. Are there unresolved issues and unfinished business still to be addressed?

_____

_____

_____

4. Are there still situations and behaviors for which you must make amends?

_____

_____

_____

5. Is there unfinished business in your life that you can't resolve? How will you let go?

_____

_____

_____

6. Think about your current relationships and issues. If not attended to in the present, will they become the unfinished business of tomorrow?

_____

_____

_____

7. What have you learned about unfinished business and recovery?

_____

_____

_____

_____

_____

8. What have you learned about yourself?

_____

_____

_____

_____

_____

THINGS TO THINK ABOUT

- Are you ready to move deeper in lifelong recovery, or do you have more work to do resolving unfinished business or making amends? Have you completed an *honest* self-appraisal in these areas?
- Are you better able to recognize unfinished business and the effects it has on your life and your recovery?

16

Destination:

THE FUTURE—

MAINTAINING RECOVERY

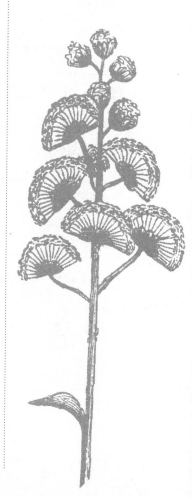

"The woods are lovely,
    dark and deep.
But I have promises to
    keep,
And miles to go before I
    sleep
And miles to go before I
    sleep."
—ROBERT FROST

TERRI

I've haven't used alcohol or drugs for over fifteen years. Although I don't regularly go to AA anymore, I still stop in from time to time to keep myself acquainted with the ideas and people of AA. I have never forgotten, nor will I, the lessons of my recovery. It took me a dozen attempts to get and stay sober, but when I finally achieved it I knew how precious and how fragile recovery is. I'll never be recovered, only in recovery.

GEORGE

Stopping addictive eating took much more than just diets. I'd lose a few pounds, then go right back to my old eating habits. It took me a long time to realize that, but once I did, I understood that it took —required—a complete change in attitude and lifestyle. It took a permanent change of self-watchfulness and self-control.

BY NOW, YOU'VE addressed many difficult and painful issues and have begun to take significant steps toward moving on with an addiction-free life. You've faced your own limitations and flaws

277

You've faced your own limitations and flaws with soul-searching honesty, and you've learned to recognize and build on your strengths.

with soul-searching honesty, and you've learned to recognize and build on your strengths. Most of all, your commitment to remain sober has resulted in a newfound humility that will serve you well in all you do. This chapter will focus on maintaining full recovery, mastering and exercising new behaviors, and applying coping and problem-solving skills.

Use the next journal entry to think about active recovery and what it means to maintain this level of recovery.

PERMANENCY PLANNING

1. Describe your perspective about addiction and recovery.

_____

_____

_____

_____

2. Describe your attitudes about abstinence and moderation.

_____

_____

_____

_____

_____

3. How conscious are you of the situations, relationships, and activities that might trigger relapse and a return to addiction?

_____

_____

_____

_____

4. How conscious are you of your own needs/cravings to engage in addictive behaviors?

_____

_____

_____

5. How committed are you to *never* returning to addiction or addictive behaviors?

_____

_____

_____

6. Do you have and are you actively using a relapse prevention plan?

_____

_____

_____

7. Are you periodically reviewing your contract for sobriety?

_____

_____

_____

8. On this 1 to 3 scale, circle the number that most approximates your responses to the following questions.

	No	Somewhat	Yes
Are you recalling *daily* the lessons learned from your addiction?	1	2	3
Are you recalling *daily* the lessons learned from your recovery?	1	2	3
Are you engaging in safe behaviors, activities, and relationships?	1	2	3
Are you remaining tuned to your thoughts and feelings?	1	2	3
Are you maintaining a healthy self-awareness?	1	2	3
Are you taking charge of and being responsible for your decisions at every level?	1	2	3

9. Are you in *active* recovery?

_____

_____

_____

_____

_____

_____

_____

THINGS TO THINK ABOUT

- Can you easily distinguish between early and active recovery?
- In Question 8, did you score 3s in each area? If not, what does this tell you?
- If you are in active recovery, what permanent lifestyle changes have you made to accommodate a permanent recovery? If you haven't made such changes, are you sure you're not still in early recovery?

Supporting Lifestyle

Developing a lifestyle that supports and strengthens an addiction-free life is imperative.

The ability to maintain recovery depends on more than just sheer willpower. Developing a lifestyle that supports and strengthens an addiction-free life is imperative.

Use the next journal entry to assess your life and lifestyle in several key areas.

THIS IS YOUR LIFE

1. On this 1 to 3 scale, circle the number that most approximates your level of functioning in each of the following areas.

	Needs Improvement	Good Shape	Great Shape
Attitudes and values that support recovery	1	2	3
Finances	1	2	3
Fun	1	2	3
Health	1	2	3
Home	1	2	3
Learning	1	2	3
People/Relationships	1	2	3
Personal interests/activities	1	2	3
Possessions	1	2	3
Self-esteem/Image	1	2	3
Service to others	1	2	3
Spirituality	1	2	3
Work/School	1	2	3

2. Describe a goal in each area for the next six months. It should be specific, measurable, and realistic (that is, achievable within six months).

Goal

Attitudes and values	_____
Finances	_____
Fun	_____
Health	_____
Home	_____
Learning	_____

Goal

People/Relationships	_____
Personal interests/activities	_____
Possessions	_____
Self-esteem/Image	_____
Service to others	_____
Spirituality	_____
Work/School	_____

3. List four obstacles that might challenge your ability to achieve these goals.

a. _____

b. _____

c. _____

d. _____

4. How would relapsing affect your future development in each area?

_____

_____

_____

_____

_____

THINGS TO THINK ABOUT

- Do you already have many of the supports needed to maintain recovery, or do you have much support building to do?
- Was it easy or difficult to set goals? Were the goals you set realistic? Were they *too* simplistic?
- Is it a good idea to develop goals for the next year and even the next five years?

Decisions and Choices

You've always had choices, and now you've exercised your choice to be addiction free. You'll face many other decisions in your life, of course, but among the most important will be those related to recovery and addictive behaviors. Your primary goal is to continue making choices that support your recovery.

Every decision you make has consequences, certainly for yourself and possibly for others. Although your choices are often limited by real-life constraints such as finances, relationships, jobs, and other matters over which you don't necessarily have full control, there are guidelines you can follow to help you make thoughtful decisions appropriate to your life. Consider these three factors.

Every decision you make has consequences, certainly for yourself and possibly for others.

1. *Responsibility.* Some decisions are not really choices at all; they are obligations. If you're a parent, for instance, you have decisions that must be made to ensure the health and safety of your children. Consider who will be affected by your decisions and for whom you may be responsible.

2. *Spontaneity versus impetuousness.* It's healthy to be spontaneous at times. Spontaneity is usually thought of as harmless and even refreshing. Impetuous behavior, however—acting without regard for consequences—is foolhardy. As you make decisions, think about the difference between being spontaneous and being impetuous. Decisions that affect your life and the lives of others should be carefully considered.

3. *Long-term effects.* Take into account that decisions you make now may have lasting effects. Changing careers or moving across town may involve some considered decision making, but neither represents a radical change. On the other hand, filing for divorce or moving to another state are far more significant decisions in terms of their long-term impact, because they are often difficult decisions to later reverse.

THINKING ABOUT DECISIONS

1. Think about *current* decisions and choices in your life. What sort of decisions are the hardest to make?

_____

_____

_____

_____

_____

2. In what way has your recovery led to the sort of choices you're now facing?

_____

_____

_____

_____

_____

3. In what ways has your recovery opened up the possibility of change?

_____

_____

_____

_____

_____

4. What sort of opportunities for change are in your life right now?

_____

_____

_____

_____

_____

5. What are the risks of change?

_____

_____

_____

_____

_____

_____

6. Who else might be affected by your decisions? In what ways?

_____

_____

_____

_____

_____

_____

THINGS TO THINK ABOUT

- Are you afraid of change or excited by it? Do your fears about change outweigh the opportunities?
- Are you at a point in your life where you can spot opportunity for change? What can you do to increase your ability to see such opportunities?
- Are you staying aware of who else might or will be affected by any major decisions you make? If so, are you discussing decisions with them?

Moving Forward

As you plan for your future, there are specific steps that can help you weigh your responsibilities and make sound decisions.

Recognize that you do have choices. You're not a passive bystander in your own life.

- *Recognize that you do have choices.* You're not a passive bystander in your own life.

- *Consider the nature of the problem that you're trying to resolve.* Every decision is a response to a particular situation: what's the issue, problem, or situation you want to address?

- *Consider all your options.* Be creative.

- *Evaluate your choices.* Determine which choices you can realistically make right now. If you are left with only one option, your decision might be made.

- *Consider all consequences.* What are the downsides to your possible decision choices? Who will be affected by your choice, and how? How will your possible choices affect your life, your finances, your relationships, and so on?

- *Reflect on your decision.* What will it feel like to actually take those steps and make that choice? What will it feel like if you reject that choice? Is the decision you're pondering permanent or reversible?

The next journal entry will help you think about individual choices and your decision-making style in general. Follow the general model for decision making described above, which is a framework you can use to map out solutions for almost any issue in your life. Copy the entry before using it if you think you may want to use it more than once.

MAKING DECISIONS

1. Briefly describe one decision you're currently pondering.

_____

2. List six different choices for resolving this issue.

a. _____   d. _____

b. _____   e. _____

c. _____   f. _____

3. Review the options you identified in Question 2, and select the three most realistic choices. Complete these sentences to describe how this choice could fit the circumstances and reality of your life.

a. *This solution fits because . . .* _____

b. *This solution fits because . . .* _____

c. *This solution fits because . . .* _____

4. Select just one of these choices, and use it as the focal point for the remainder of this entry.

_____

5. What are the possible consequences of this choice? Is there a price to pay?

_____

_____

_____

_____

6. How will your life be affected by this choice?

_____

_____

_____

_____

_____

7. Who else's life will be affected by this decision, and how?

_____

_____

_____

_____

THINGS TO THINK ABOUT

- Do you better understand the issues and choices involved in this decision? What stops you from making a choice and acting on it?
- Can you afford to take a chance on this decision, or are the consequences irreversible?
- Are you acting too quickly on decisions without giving them ample thought, or are you not acting quickly enough?

Looking Forward by Looking Back

Before turning to this book's final chapter, take a few minutes to reflect on the journey you've made through addiction and to recovery.

REFLECTIONS ON YOUR JOURNEY

1. *I've most learned . . .* _____

_____

_____

_____

_____

2. As I look back on my recovery and renewal work, I . . . _____

_____

_____

_____

_____

_____

3. My journey through recovery has left me feeling . . . _____

_____

_____

_____

_____

4. The most bitter part of my journey has been . . . _____

_____

_____

_____

_____

5. The best part of my journey has been . . . _____

_____

_____

_____

_____

6. I most need to say . . . _____

_____

_____

_____

_____

7. What one thing could you do differently that would most improve the quality of your life?

_____

_____

_____

_____

THINGS TO THINK ABOUT

- Has this entry helped you put your recovery into perspective and recognize what's behind and what's ahead?
- What will it take for you to really feel that the issues, anxieties, and fears raised by addiction are resolved? Will those feelings ever completely go away?
- What has this journey taught you about yourself and your life in general?

17

As One Journey Ends, Another Begins

THE END OF this journal does not mark the end of your recovery process. That will continue throughout your life. What you've been through and what you've learned from your journaling work *will* set the pace for your journey still ahead. If your experience with recovery has left you wiser, stronger, and more confident than ever, you're in good shape. If, however, your journey has left you emotionally shaky and uncertain, consider tapping back into your support system to get the help you need.

If you've come this far in *The Healing Journey Through Addiction,* then you've found value in the journaling process. Will your journal continue to be a useful tool and valuable companion as you continue along your lifelong journey? The final journal entry will help you answer that question.

MY JOURNAL

1. How has your journal been most useful?

_____

_____

_____

_____

_____

2. Have certain types of journal entries been more useful than others? Explain.

_____

_____

_____

_____

_____

3. What's been the most difficult aspect of journaling for you?

_____

_____

_____

_____

4. What's been the most fulfilling aspect of journaling?

_____

_____

_____

_____

5. Overall, describe your experience keeping this journal.

_____

_____

_____

_____

_____

_____

6. *My journal* . . . _____

_____

_____

_____

_____

_____

_____

_____

_____

_____

THINGS TO THINK ABOUT

- Have you enjoyed keeping a journal? If you've kept a journal before, what was different about this journal?
- Will you continue to use a journal in the future? If so, will you only keep a journal under special circumstances, or will you keep a daily journal?

In completing this book you've accomplished a great deal and have taken significant steps down the path to self-help and personal growth. One thing that we have learned in writing this book (and we hope that you too have learned this in the process of giving up your addiction) is this: no one can do it for us, but neither can we do it alone.

Think about who helped you in the process of recovery. Each of us owes deep thanks to those who have rekindled our inner light. Write a short note of thanks to those who have helped you, and commit yourself to being of help to those who are taking similar journeys.

Acknowledgments

From Stu: I acknowledge my debt to Jean Kinney, whose invitation to lecture, then write, then cartoon about addictions was the beginning of what has been a lifelong pursuit; to the staff, patients, and parents of Osgood 3, who taught me far more about addiction and recovery than I taught them; and especially to Nick, Elisabeth, and Jill; to Stuart Matlins, publisher, editor, and unacknowledged coauthor of *Twelve Jewish Steps to Recovery* and to Rabbi Kerry Olitski, who showed me that religion and spirituality were not incompatible; to David Shneyer and the Fabrengen Fiddlers, whose music, though addicting, is purely a positive addiction; to Phil Rich, who takes my simple thoughts and extracts them from my all too frequently all too complicated, all too complex, and far too long sentences; and to Kelly Franklin, whose vision helped create a series where we had only envisioned a book. If, as some have suggested, every act of creation is in fact an act of collaboration, I have been fortunate in my collaborators, who are wise, learned, holy, and dedicated to helping others.

From Phil: My deepest thanks to my wife, Bev Sevier, who has helped me keep on the right track and make the best decisions I can and to my lovely daughter, Kaye Sevier, who has helped keep my inner light alive. Thanks also to Stu Copans, a good writing partner and a very good friend, who has really helped stimulate and challenge my thinking and my creativity. Always many thanks to Kelly Franklin, our publisher at John Wiley & Sons, for bringing The Healing Journey series to life. And thanks to our editor, Tracey Belmont, and the other Wiley production staff who have worked on this and all the other Healing Journey books, as well as Christine Cleveland and the folks at Running Feet Books.